GW01149672

THE GIVING WORLD

THE GIVING WORLD

The three financial forces that could transform global development

Mona Hammami Hijazi

THINKERS 50

Copyright © Mona Hammami Hijazi, 2016

The right of Mona Hammami Hijazi to be identified as the author of this book has been asserted in accordance with the Copyright, Designs and Patents Act 1988.

First published in 2016 by
Infinite Ideas Limited
36 St Giles
Oxford
OX1 3LD
United Kingdom
www.infideas.com

All rights reserved. Except for the quotation of small passages for the purposes of criticism or review, no part of this publication may be reproduced, stored in a retrieval system or transmitted in any form or by any means, electronic, mechanical, photocopying, recording, scanning or otherwise, except under the terms of the Copyright, Designs and Patents Act 1988 or under the terms of a licence issued by the Copyright Licensing Agency Ltd, 90 Tottenham Court Road, London W1T 4LP, UK, without the permission in writing of the publisher. Requests to the publisher should be addressed to the Permissions Department, Infinite Ideas Limited, 36 St Giles, Oxford, OX1 3LD, UK, or faxed to +44 (0) 1865 514777.

A CIP catalogue record for this book is available from the British Library

ISBN 978–1–908984–32–6

Brand and product names are trademarks or registered trademarks of their respective owners.

Printed in Dubai

Contents

Foreword by Robin Niblett	*vii*
Introduction	1
PART 1 – SMART AID	17
1. Aid matters	19
2. The rise of the new donors	29
3. Does aid work?	39
4. Towards an aid strategy	43
5. An aid roadmap	71
PART II – CHANGING LIVES THROUGH REMITTANCES	79
6. Migration and remittances – trends and flows	81
7. Remittances – benefits and risks	89
8. Sending money home	95
9. More effective remittances – the role of government policy	105
10. A remittances roadmap	121
PART III – PHILANTHROPY FOR IMPACT	125
11. The philanthropists	129
12. How philanthropy works	139
13. Philanthropy 2.0 – the evolving value chain	151
14. Proactive government	159

15. A philanthropy roadmap 177

Conclusion – the transformation agenda 181
Glossary 189
About the author 191
Acknowledgments 193
Notes 195
Index 207

Foreword

2015 was a pivotal year for international development and the future alleviation of poverty. Governments came together at the UN General Assembly in September and adopted the '2030 Agenda for Sustainable Development', thereby confirming their commitment to build upon the successful achievement of a number of the Millennium Development Goals. The new Agenda will sustain momentum towards the eradication of poverty and hunger, promote healthier lives, and help societies adopt a more gender-inclusive and environmentally aware approach to national and international economic growth. Especially notable was the fact that all governments, whether developed, middle income, or developing, signed up to the agenda. This reflected the dramatic rebalancing of global economic power that has taken place over the past twenty years, and the increasingly shared nature of the challenges to sustainable growth faced by countries throughout the world.

At the same time, the commitments made in 2015 are now running into the headwinds of a worldwide slowdown in economic growth. Governments from countries as diverse as China, Turkey, Brazil, and South Africa have embarked on the difficult process of assisting their people transition into middle-income status. This transition is proving to be difficult, as the economic travails of all four during 2015 made clear. Systems of governance that oversaw major infrastructure investment and export-led growth are attempting to adjust to the very different needs of businesses delivering services and to the expectations of better-informed populations. The collapse of the commodity boom, which has affected negatively a number of economies dependent on commodity exports for their growth, reflects in part this less energy- and resource-intensive profile of future economic growth. It also reflects a world that is coming to terms with the commitments at the United Nations Climate Change Conference Paris Summit of December 2015 to reduce significantly the carbon intensity of future economic growth. Whether they are commodity importers or exporters, governments across the world are struggling to adjust to this new normal.

The question arises, therefore, of whether the growing diversification of sources of developmental funding, which expanded in the late 1990s and first decade of the twenty-first century from the developed, Western world (including countries such as Japan and Australia) to the rising economic powers, such as China, India, and Brazil, can be sustained. At the same time, governments in the West are struggling under the high debt overhang from the global financial crisis of 2008–10 and with populations that have lost trust in their governments' ability to sustain a continued steady growth in their standards of living, whether because of the belt tightening that followed the crash or because of the gradual erosion of their economic competitiveness in a globalized economy.

It is in this complex context that Mona Hammami Hijazi sets out her thoughts and insights in this book on the future of developmental assistance, which comprises the broad set of funding sources and mechanisms whereby outside actors – whether governments, private foundations, or individuals – seek to help countries and societies improve their economic opportunities in ways that are economically, socially, and environmentally sustainable. But rather than focus on one specific dimension, *The Giving World* brings together under one cover an analysis of the three principal but distinct pillars of development assistance – official development assistance (ODA) by governments, as defined by the OECD; remittances by workers to their families; and the investments made by diverse strands of philanthropy, from high-net-worth individuals to major foundations to campaigns funded by tens or hundreds of thousands of mobilized individuals. By unpicking each of these three strands and analyzing their potential, their achievements and shortfalls, Mona Hammami Hijazi lays out the differences in their origins and motivation, while also making clear to the reader the interconnections between them. Despite the growing economic and internal political pressures on donor countries and communities described above, these interconnections offer the potential for developmental assistance to play an even more important role in supporting the new Agenda for Sustainable Development than it did during the pursuit of the Millennium Development Goals.

The book's most important contribution is to describe how governments must play a central role in ensuring that developmental assistance, whether sourced from tighter central government funds or from ever more inventive and entrepreneurial private sources, achieves its maximum positive impact. Strategic planning, legislative and legal frameworks, implementation methods, and monitoring practices are all essential elements on effective developmental assistance. Governmental planning can also enhance the impact of private sources of funding, which, in the case of remittances, amounted to some $580 billion in 2014 alone.

Overall, *The Giving World* highlights how good governance plays as critical a role in successful development assistance as it does in the ability of developing countries to absorb, benefit from, and leverage the funds that they receive. If the world is to look back in fifteen years' time at the accomplishments of the 2030 Agenda for Sustainable Development and experience some of the same satisfaction as it did from the experience of the MDGs, then governments will need to adapt, upgrade, and modernize their thinking along the lines proposed in the course of the following chapters.

Robin Niblett
Director, Chatham House

Introduction

As many observers have noted we are living in a world that is volatile, uncertain, complex, and ambiguous.

On one hand, it is a world where there is great progress. A world in transition, where billions of people are on the move: from rural to urban, village to cities and megacities, agrarian to industrial to technological, poor to middle income, developing economy to developed economy. Millions of migrants are searching for – and finding – a better life.

Yet, at the same time, and despite our advances, there remain many challenges. Wicked problems. The world suffers from huge developmental issues. Poverty, hunger, water scarcity, disease, high infant mortality, and illiteracy are all part of everyday reality for billions of people.

But while these challenges may seem daunting, they are not insoluble. Great progress has been made already – just look at the achievements in working towards the United Nations Millennium Development Goals – and we can make much more.

Well-designed developmental programs can help build urban environments, provide infrastructure, relieve poverty, increase food and water security, cope with humanitarian crises, and combat climate change. But, here we come to the crunch: progress is costly. Even when there is the will, resources are often lacking.

This is where three forms of development finance which often receive little attention can help make a difference. They have the potential to transform the developing world: aid, remittances, and philanthropy.

Individually and collectively these three flows of money represent an unprecedented transfer of wealth. Together they make up what one could describe as 'givin-omics' – the giving ecosystem. Maximizing these three powerful financial forces has the power to change the world for the better and is the focus of *The Giving World*.

This is not hyperbole. To get an idea of the scale of these transfers, consider the following. In 2014 donors provided $135.2 billion in net official development assistance.[1] In the same year, an estimated $583 billion remittances were transferred globally; and in the US alone some $358.4 billion was given to charities through philanthropy. Used wisely, these relatively untapped elements have the power to transform the world. Moreover, these three sources of finance are rarely, if ever, considered together. Until now.

The Giving World examines the three forces of aid, remittances, and philanthropy in detail. A separate part of the book is devoted to each. Part I looks at aid; Part II examines remittances; and Part III investigates the changing face of philanthropy.

Each of the three financial forces is considered in the light of important shifts taking place in the world, and a roadmap is provided to make them a more effective means of distributing much-needed money and resources and achieving intended goals.

Most importantly, the book considers how we can harness the power of these three forces, and in particular the role that governments and other private parties can play in maximizing the use and effectiveness of this tidal wave of money. Each section provides a useful checklist of the actions and decisions that governments should be thinking about to maximize the effectiveness of these financial flows.

A WORLD IN FLUX

The huge potential power of aid, remittances, and philanthropy should not detract from the magnitude and multitude of the challenges faced by the peoples of the world and their governments.

For a start there is great inequality. A report by Credit Suisse found that the richest 1 percent of the world's population now owns 50 percent of its total wealth.[2] Much of the wealth of the world resides with a fortunate few, while many others possess very little. Poverty blights the lives of millions. In 2012, 896 million people, 12.7 percent of the world's population, were living at or below the global poverty line of $1.90 a day.[3]

Hand in hand with poverty go hunger and malnourishment. While millions need to do little more than go to the supermarket or the kitchen cupboard for their food, millions more eke out their existence close to starvation, never knowing for sure where the next meal will come from. Some 795 million people remained undernourished in 2015.[4] Over 90 million of the undernourished and underweight were children aged under five.

Poverty and hunger are invariably associated with poor health. For many people living in the developing world, the doctor does not visit when they are ill. Often there are no doctors within tens of miles. There are no local hospitals. According to the World Health Organization at least a billion people suffer every year from being unable to obtain the health services they need. Many people are simply unable to afford basic services that people in the developed world take for granted. It is calculated that about 150 million people are financially ruined through accessing healthcare, and 100 million pushed below the poverty line.[5]

Diseases, such as HIV/AIDS and malaria, are rife in some parts of the world. In 2013, it was estimated that 35 million people were living with HIV. Yet the number of people receiving antiretroviral therapy (ART) globally was less than half that at 13.6 million. Significant progress has been made in combatting malaria, yet in 2013 there were roughly 198 million cases of malaria and 584,000 deaths. In Africa, according to the World Health Organization, a child dies every minute from the disease.[6]

Many children never get the chance to live a long, happy, healthy, and productive life. Their lives are destined to be short. In 2015, some 16,000 children under five died every day, mostly from preventable causes. Expectant mothers suffer too. In 2013 there were an estimated 289,000 maternal deaths globally. Each day 800 women die from preventable causes related to pregnancy or childbirth.[7]

Many people can simply turn on a tap and clean, drinkable water pours out when they are thirsty. Unfortunately this is far from reality for billions of people around the world. In 2015 an estimated 663 million people used drinking water that came from an unimproved source as classified by the WHO/UNICEF joint monitoring program, such as unprotected springs, unprotected dug wells, and surface water. Nearly half of these people lived in Sub-Saharan Africa, and a fifth in Southern Asia.[8]

While four out of five people in urban areas had access to piped water on their premises, in rural areas only a third of the population had similar access. In addition, 42 percent of people in Sub-Saharan Africa lived further than 500 meters from an improved water source, such as piped water, a borehole, or a protected spring.[9]

Understandably, where safe water is scarce, sanitation is often poor as well. Some 2.4 billion people lacked improved sanitation facilities in 2015, as described by WHO/UNICEF, with 13 percent of the global population, and 25 percent of those living in rural areas, still having to defecate in the open. In countries such as Uganda and Liberia, less than 10 percent of the population had a hand-washing facility at home with soap and water. In Bangladesh only a quarter of the population had these facilities, and in Pakistan just over half.[10]

At the same time the governments of the world are battling climate change, which presents a serious challenge to the future wellbeing of the planet. As pointed out in a presentation to the UN of the IPCC's Fifth Assessment Report, the human influence on the climate is clear and there are real risks of pervasive and irreversible impacts. These include greater temperature extremes, warmer oceans, shrinking Arctic sea ice and glacier cover, significant rises in sea levels, and more severe storms. The effects of climate change will displace thousands of people, and further exacerbate poverty levels and food and water shortages.[11]

In addition there are a number of humanitarian crises playing out at any particular moment. An outbreak of the hemorrhagic disease Ebola began in Guinea, West Africa, in December 2013. By early 2014 it had spread to neighboring Liberia and Sierra Leone. It took until August for WHO to designate the outbreak a Public Health Emergency of International Concern, while in September the UN Security Council declared it 'a threat to international peace and security'. After a concerted and rapid aid effort, the spread of Ebola was contained primarily within Liberia, Sierra Leone, and Guinea, with a small number of cases in Nigeria and Mali, and isolated incidents in the US, Italy, UK, Senegal, and Spain. Over 11,000 people died, a figure that is believed to be under-reported; the economic impact was significant; and, almost two years after the outbreak began, there were still a small number of cases being reported every week in Guinea.[12]

More recently a refugee crisis arising from conflict in Syria has prompted an emergency response in Europe. As of October 2015, some four million refugees had been registered as persons of concern.[13] With many more unregistered, and hundreds of thousands of refugees making their way to and across Europe, this is a still-unfolding humanitarian crisis.

There are periodic natural disasters, too, that cause widespread devastation and untold misery, prompting a humanitarian response. Take the April 2015 earthquake in Nepal, for example, which killed nearly 9,000 people and injured more than 20,000.[14]

Another global trend is set to exacerbate many of these problems. The world's population is expanding rapidly. It took over 100,000 years for the earth's population to reach one billion. Since that moment, in 1804, population growth has accelerated, passing the two billion mark in the 1930s and reaching seven billion in 2011. By 2062 the world may well be home to ten billion people on current projections. And the UN has calculated that by 2100, according to the 'high variant' – one of three possible scenarios it considered – there could be as many as 17 billion people living on this planet.[15]

This population growth is not evenly distributed, either. Much of it will be in Asia and Africa. Between now and 2050 Africa will welcome a projected 1.3 billion people to the world. The populations of over 28 countries are expected to double.[16] Most of these people will be in the poorest region, Sub-Saharan Africa.

Accompanying substantial increases in population is increased urbanization. More people mean more cities. (The rural population will grow too, but reach its peak around 2020.) The urban population exceeded the rural population in 2010. If forecasts are correct, two-thirds of humanity will be living in cities by 2050. Many of these cities will be teeming with people. Megacities with populations well in excess of 10 million will number 41 or more by 2030, compared with 28 today.[17]

More people, living in greater numbers of larger cities, will inevitably put increased pressure on the world's resources. At present it takes 1.5 years to replace the resources that we consume in one year. We exceed what nature can provide by more than half. At the current pace we would need three times what the earth is capable of producing in one year by 2050.[18]

THE WORLD'S RESPONSE

The extent of the world's challenges is clear, and a concern. It is the reality of living in the twenty-first century for billions of people; the context within which governments strive to do the best for their populations. Fortunately, the world has not been idle in the face of these many challenges. It may have taken some time, and the response is not always concerted, but many nations are trying to address these challenges.

A good example of collective action at work in an attempt to solve some of the world's more pressing problems is the UN Millennium Development Goals. World leaders gathered at the beginning of the new millennium to discuss how, together, they could battle global poverty. The result was eight ambitious goals, backed by 21 targets and 60 official indicators, with a concluding date of 31 December 2015.

The goals addressed a range of issues: eradicating extreme poverty and hunger; achieving universal primary education; promoting gender equality; reducing child mortality; improving maternal health; combatting HIV/AIDS, malaria and other diseases; and ensuring environmental sustainability.

The results have been impressive, but uneven. Between 1990 and 2015 the number of people living in extreme poverty decreased by over 50 percent from 1.9 billion to 836 million. Most of this decline happened post-2000. Equally, the proportion of undernourished people in the developing world fell by almost a half from 1990 to 2015, from 23.3 to 12.9 percent.[19]

More children are attending primary school, with the net enrolment numbers up to 91 percent in 2015, from 83 percent in 2000. At the same time the number of primary school age children *not* attending school has fallen to 57 million from 100 million.[20]

Progress has also been made on health. Vaccination programs have helped to bring down cases of measles by some 67 percent between 2000 and 2013, preventing an estimated 15.6 million deaths. Child mortality in infants under the age of five was reduced from 90 to 43 deaths per 1000 live births. Maternal mortality ratios are also substantially down from their 1990 figures; by half worldwide from 1990 to 2014, and by 64 percent in Southern Asia.[21]

Both malaria and tuberculosis are diseases that have inflicted huge suffering on mankind over many centuries. However, in recent years many millions of lives have been spared as a result of efforts to meet the Millennium Development Goals. The incidence of malaria fell by some 37 percent between 2000 and 2015, and the mortality rate by over half. Between 2000 and 2013, the tuberculosis mortality rate fell by 45 percent. With HIV/AIDS the situation has also improved. Treatment of HIV with antiretroviral therapy increased from just 800,000 in 2003 to over 13.5 million by the middle of 2014.[22]

More people have access to safe drinking water and better sanitation as a result of the millennium goals. At least 90 percent of the world's population had access to an improved water source in 2010, compared with around 76 percent in 1990, and 2.1 billion people have obtained access to improved sanitation. These statistics are testimony to what is possible, given the will and the resources.

However, as the UN acknowledges and as highlighted earlier in this introduction, despite the progress made, much more remains to be achieved. At the UN Sustainable Development Summit held in New York in September 2015, a new program, 'Transforming Our World: The 2030 Agenda for Sustainable Development' was adopted. This consists of 17 sustainable development goals. Many of these are very ambitious, not least the goals of ending poverty in all its forms everywhere (Goal 1); ending hunger, achieving food security and improved nutrition, and promoting sustainable agriculture (Goal 2); and ensuring healthy lives and promoting wellbeing for all at all ages (Goal 3).

As well as these noble aims, the 17 goals cover issues focused on in the Millennium Development Goals, such as education, gender equality, water and sanitation, and climate change. But they also take in new areas such as employment and economic growth, cities and human settlements, inequality, peace and justice, and infrastructure, industrialization, and innovation.

PARTNERS IN PROGRESS

The achievements made in areas covered by the Millennium Development Goals owe much to the cooperative and coordinated efforts of a range of stakeholders. From the governments of the most powerful countries in the world to the smallest NGOs, from intergovernmental institutions to multinational corporations, from high-net-worth philanthropists and their foundations to small individual donors, all have contributed to the gains that have been made.

The UN knew that it would be difficult for nations to make headway and achieve the goals without working in partnership with many other bodies. It recognized this in its eighth goal: 'Develop a global partnership for development'. This covered five substantive areas: market access, in terms of international trade; debt sustainability, including qualification for debt relief; access to affordable medicines; access to new technologies, including cell phones and the internet; and finally, official development assistance, and in particular focusing on a target of allotting 0.7 percent of gross national income (GNI) to ODA (Official Development Assistance).

In reaffirming the 0.7 percent target for ODA, the UN recognized the undisputed fact that any progress towards the millennium goals would cost money. A lot of money. The World Bank, using a number of different methods, calculated that 'if countries improve their policies and institutions, the additional foreign aid required to reach the Millennium Development Goals by 2015 is between $40 and $60 billion a year'.[23]

It is also worth noting that one of the co-authors of the original World Bank paper, Shanta Devarajan, the World Bank's chief economist for the Middle East and North Africa, later questioned the estimates and methods used to arrive at them.[24] In doing so Devarajan made a number of points. One was that, in estimating costs, attention is shifted from the difficult matter of policy reform in order to achieve goals to the question of funding: from innovation to accounting. Or, as he puts it: 'By starting with the costs, the discussion of all the policy and institutional reforms needed to accelerate progress – not to mention make the additional resources productive – became an add-on rather than the centerpiece of the debate.'

He also noted that it would be wrong for governments to allow a focus on the financing needed to avoid undertaking the policy reforms required to achieve the Millennium Development Goals, many of which are politically difficult and inconvenient.

Nevertheless, it would also be wrong to ignore the fact that large amounts of funds were and still are required, both to achieve the Millennium Development Goals, and to strive towards the post-2015 objectives. Some estimates of the cost of reaching the new sustainable development goals are in excess of $100 trillion.[25] [26]

In addition, there are the costs associated with increased urbanization. Infrastructure spending, for example, is set to rise to $9 trillion, driven in part by rapid urbanization, particularly in Asia. In just 20 years, China's building-space construction is equivalent to the entire territory of the Netherlands. In one year alone China built more residential floor space than all the residential building stock in Australia.

The 2030 Agenda for Sustainable Development acknowledges the role of national parliaments, through legislation and budgets, and in implementation through working closely 'with regional and local authorities, sub-regional institutions, international institutions, academia, philanthropic organizations, volunteer groups and others'.

The Agenda imagines a 'revitalized Global Partnership' bringing together 'governments, the private sector, civil society, the United Nations system and other actors and mobilizing all available resources'.

And those resources will include international public finance, including Official Development Assistance, with the target of 0.7 percent of ODA/GNI to developing countries and 0.15 percent to 0.2 percent of ODA/GNI to the least developed countries.

But ODA will not be enough. After all, the 2015 report of the Millennium Development Goals Gap Task Force identified a considerable shortfall between the ODA commitment enshrined in the eighth goal and current reality. Of the $326 billion that should have been raised (by the OECD Development Assistance Committee countries), only $135 billion was delivered in 2014, equivalent to 0.29 percent of developed-country combined gross national income. This left a gap, more of a chasm, of $191 billion.

And global economics and domestic politics are likely to act as a constraint on ODA spending in many countries. There is a very real risk that the global economy is entering an extended period of low growth. An aging population in developed economies and low productivity in emerging economies may contribute to what has been termed 'secular stagnation' (the origins of the term are attributed to US economist Alvin Hansen in the 1930s). This is where inflation is so low that the usual policy of lowering interest rates to stimulate growth becomes ineffective.

At the same time the world is racking up huge amounts of debt. For example, according to the McKinsey Global Institute, total world debt increased by $57 trillion between 2007 and 2014, growing at an average of 5.3 percent per year. A particular worry is that many emerging economies have taken on massive amounts of dollar-dominated debt while money has been relatively cheap. Add in the fact that many corporations are highly leveraged, and the conditions are there for another credit crunch.

Growth is slowing in China, Brazil is in recession, and many other emerging countries are suffering economically for a variety of reasons. These countries rely on inflows of foreign capital. Should the capital dry up, possibly because of an external event such as the hiking of interest rates in the US, then there could be serious funding problems.

But while ODA may suffer in the short to mid term, there are still significant flows of funding besides ODA which are likely to be directed towards achieving the sustainable development goals and other major problems, global and regional, faced by different governments. The UN's Report of the Intergovernmental Committee of Experts on Sustainable Development Financing makes a number of policy recommendations which, taken together, 'can have a powerful impact by redirecting flows towards financing sustainable development'.[27]

The flows that the report focuses on are domestic public, domestic private, international public, international private finance, and blended finance. As the report notes, international financial flows to developing countries have increased rapidly in the last ten years.

Much of this increase has been as a result of growth in remittances. These private cross-border transfers of money to developing countries from migrants back to their homes and communities amounted to an estimated $404 billion in 2013. In 1990 the amount was less than $40 billion.[28] A large proportion of the global population is on the move; between 2000 and 2015 some 4.6 million migrants a year traveled from lower and middle economies to higher income countries. The more people improve their position through migration, the greater the flow and value of remittances to developing countries. This already rivals or exceeds foreign direct investment in some cases.

Another significant source of domestic and cross-border finance is philanthropic finance. These funds may originate from private individuals, both the very wealthy and those of more moderate means, philanthropic foundations, and other organizations. In 2013 they represented some $60 billion, much of it from private donors in the developed economies.[29]

Together these three sources of funding – aid, remittances, and philanthropic finance – can make a big contribution towards meeting development goals, relieving the financial stress from population growth and increased urbanization, and alleviating humanitarian crises. It is these three sources of funding that *The Giving World* focuses on.

WHEN THREE RIVERS MEET

The power of aid, remittances, and philanthropy when they work together is enormous and proven. At the headquarters of the World Bank in Washington DC, there is a statue of a child leading a blind man. The same statue can be seen at the offices of the World Health Organization in Geneva; the New Jersey HQ of the multinational pharmaceutical giant Merck; and in Amsterdam at the Royal Tropical Institute of the Netherlands. The distinctive statue is also to be found in Atlanta, Georgia, at the Carter Center, and in Ouagadougou, the capital of the African country of Burkina Faso. It is a reminder of the proud part each has played in the fight to control one of Africa's most devastating diseases, onchocerciasis, better known as river blindness.[30]

The Onchocerciasis Control Program has rightly earned its place as one of the great achievements of international public health. It is testament to the power of collaboration across countries and agencies, the vital role of long-term funding from the donor community, and the benefits of public and private partnership in bringing a medical innovation to transform the lives of the people who need it most.

Onchocerciasis is a debilitating disease that afflicts around 25 million people worldwide, mostly (99 percent) in Sub-Saharan Africa, but also in Latin America and Yemen. In the worst affected areas, a large proportion of the adult population is either blind or infected with the disease. River blindness is caused by a worm which enters its human victim through the bite of an infected blackfly. In areas where the fly breeds, residents are bitten as many as 10,000 times a day. Inside its human host, the tiny worm grows to two to three feet in length, producing millions of microscopic offspring. The worms' movement causes unbearable itching, skin lesions, rashes, muscle pain, weakness, and, in the most severe cases, blindness.

Today, an estimated 300,000 people are blind as a result of the disease, and 800,000 million are severely visually impaired.[31] As well as the dreadful toll of human suffering, the disease has a pernicious economic impact — reducing the income of families, the marriage prospects of individuals, and increasing health costs. It has also led to more than 250,000 square kilometers of the best arable land in West Africa being abandoned.

Early attempts to control the disease met with mixed results and by the late 1960s it became apparent that it could only be controlled if it was addressed on a sufficiently large scale. But, despite the preparation of a regional control plan, it was difficult to obtain adequate funding commitments for a 20-year, $20 million program, across seven countries.

Eventually, in 1972, after witnessing the devastation caused by river blindness at first hand in West Africa, Robert McNamara, then president of the World Bank, decided to lead an international effort to combat the disease. He also committed the World Bank to help finance it. The Onchocerciasis Control Program (OCP) was launched in 1974 under the leadership of the WHO, the World Bank, the Food and Agriculture Organization (FAO), and the United Nations Development Program (UNDP).

The fight against onchocerciasis received a boost when the pharmaceutical company Merck discovered that Mectizan, a treatment for gastrointestinal worms in cattle and horses, was also effective against the family of worms responsible for onchocerciasis. Crucially, too, the new drug could be administered in one dose, rather than requiring multiple doses like other treatments for tropical diseases.

In its quest for a partner organization to help organize and fund the distribution of this drug Merck turned to Dr William Foege, executive director at the Carter Center, a nonprofit public policy center founded by Jimmy and Rosalynn Carter to fight disease, hunger, poverty, conflict, and oppression around the world. In 1987, Ray Vagelos, CEO of Merck, made the historic announcement that his company would donate Mectizan 'to anyone who needed it, for as long as it was needed'.

Today the efforts of the OCP, the Carter Center, and Merck, and numerous other initiatives, have made a significant impact on the incidence and spread of river blindness. ODA funding, such as the Canadian International Development Agency's (CIDA) support for the African Program for Onchocerciasis Control, has contributed. So have philanthropists, both through Foundations and Centers such as the Carter Center, as well as individually – a $1 million donation came from a Nigerian survivor of river blindness, General Theophilus Danjuma.[32] [33]

Remittances too, have played an important role in alleviating suffering from river blindness. In Burkino Faso, for example, cultivation of fertile river basin valleys in the country's south-central and south-western regions was impossible due to endemic river blindness. Many displaced Burkinabé workers traveled to neighboring Côte d'Ivoire, sending back remittances to support their families.[34] [35]

The success of the OCP program is striking. At the start of the program in 1974, for example, nearly 2.5 million of the 30 million people in the area were infected and 100,000 of them were blind. Today transmission of the disease has been virtually halted, and some 1.5 million people who were once infected no longer experience any symptoms. An estimated 600,000 cases of blindness have been prevented and 22 million children born in the area since the program began are free from the risk of river blindness.

The economic impact has also been impressive. With the removal of the threat of the disease, an estimated 25 million hectares of arable land has been made available – with the potential to feed an additional 17 million people.

While much has been achieved through the use of ODA, remittances, and philanthropic finance in treating onchocerciasis and elsewhere, much more is possible. And, although two of the sources of funding – remittances and philanthropic finance – are private, governments of the world have a vital role both in encouraging the donation of these financial flows and ensuring that they are used in the most effective way, achieving the best possible outcomes.

At present, these huge sums of money are underutilized, falling far short of their potential maximum impact. One reason is that the transfers of money related to remittances and philanthropy – partly because of their private nature – rarely attract the attention and resources that they deserve. As a result they are poorly understood and there is little coordination or dissemination of best practice, unlike other areas of financial and economic policy such as foreign direct investment.

NAVIGATING THE BOOK

The issues associated with aid, remittances, and philanthropic financial flows are rarely examined together in one book. Yet, in the modern world these different types of international giving (income transfers) cannot be considered entirely distinct. If governments want to maximize the impact of these three flows then they need to consider them independently – but also collectively, leveraging any synergies. Governments have a role to play related to all three.

Governments need a shift in focus. Fully understood, and with a coordinated policy to maximize their effectiveness, these flows of funds represent a powerful resource for driving social and economic change.

Drawing on information from multiple research sources and documents, this book investigates how governments can approach this issue holistically, exploring the interactions and synergies between the three types of financial transfer, in order to derive greater benefits.

The Giving World is divided into four main parts. Part I: Smart aid looks at aid, its history, aid mechanisms, good practice, and current trends. The landscape of aid is changing. The influence of countries that have historically dominated aid may be waning, while new donors, previously the recipients of aid, are shaking up the way aid is delivered and the motivation for providing it. As these roles change, the effectiveness of aid strategy under the different models is explored.

Part II – Changing lives through remittances – examines the flow of money from millions of migrant workers back to their families and communities. Traditionally this transfer of wealth has mostly been in the form of individual remittances. Money is sent back to families to help pay for food and shelter or is deposited in a bank in the worker's home country, as a kind of self-funded social security. More recently, though, migrants are pooling money collectively, earmarking funds for the development in their communities. The book explores the ways in which policymakers, in both donor and recipient countries, can encourage migrants to make remittances, and leverage remittances as a tool for dealing with social and economic issues.

Then in Part III, Philanthropy for impact, attention is turned to philanthropy and the huge amounts donated by individuals and organizations. While the billions of dollars given under the broad umbrella of philanthropy may appear to have little to do with government, the reality could be very different. Philanthropy is changing. A new generation of philanthropists is applying a range of entrepreneurship tools and strategies to their philanthropic endeavors. Governments can tap into this new trend and help to incentivize and facilitate more strategic philanthropic giving.

Each part highlights both trends and best practice. And, in addition, the three main sections provide a practical framework for all those stakeholders engaged in maximizing the outcomes from these three financial flows. What should government's overarching strategic approach be?

Finally, in the Conclusion: The transformation agenda, we examine the interaction between these three financial flows. Where is the common ground in the frameworks and strategic approach adopted for each source of funds? What are the lessons for governments, policymakers, and others concerned with maximizing the impact of these different types of transfer of money, in any donor or recipient country? What new roles are there for governments, where traditionally they have not ventured beyond regulatory control?

Despite the challenges the world faces, I remain optimistic about the future. Mankind is resolute, resilient, and resourceful. My aim is that this book will provide the many stakeholders committed to making our world a better place with a unique and different perspective on the issues involved. Hopefully, it will inspire them to create radical and innovative solutions to the many challenges that society faces.

Part 1

Smart aid

The concept of foreign aid dates back to the early nineteenth century at least and the 1812 Act for the Relief of the Citizens of Venezuela, passed by the American Congress. However, it was only comparatively recently, in the late twentieth century, that a concerted effort was made to harmonize the definition of development assistance and efforts to establish best practice and standards.

The work of the Development Assistance Committee has forced governments to work together to address some of the problems associated with aid provision. At the same time it has gone some way to improving the effectiveness of aid.

However, the aid landscape is changing rapidly. The lines between countries traditionally perceived as recipients of aid and those considered donors, the North-South divide, are increasingly blurred. New donors are emerging, such as China, with their own ideas about what aid should look like.

It seems clear that there is no universal blueprint for managing aid, no magic model. But there are some characteristics of a government's approach to aid, discussed in the following section, that are likely to enhance the impact of that aid. They include setting clear objectives; having well defined targets in terms of the recipients of aid; having a clear governance structure coordinating between different aid donors; and monitoring and regularly evaluating the impact of aid.

This section is not about recommending a particular aid model or approach. Instead it is about providing an understanding of the aid ecosystem and the constituent elements of an aid program, plus a roadmap that can be used to help devise an effective aid strategy.

In so doing it looks at some aid successes, the modern history of aid, definitions and trends, challenges, and approaches.

1
Aid matters

The value of Official Development Assistance should never be underestimated. Around the world ODA helps to improve the lives of millions of people. It eases the fiscal burden of the countries receiving aid and helps them to accomplish projects and programs from major infrastructure projects to small community programs. ODA might have also helped some countries attain the Millennium Development Goals.

Benefits commonly attributed to aid include the stimulation of economic growth through infrastructure building; the support of productive sectors such as agriculture; the introduction of new ideas and technologies; strengthening social outcomes such as education, health, and social safety nets; supporting the subsistence consumption of food and other commodities, especially during relief operations and humanitarian interventions; and stabilizing economies following economic shocks.

Development aid has made a huge difference in the world. It has helped to alleviate many of the world's most challenging problems.

Take food security and hunger, for example. Food shortages have haunted mankind throughout its history. The ever-constant threat of famine cast a long shadow over the lives of our ancestors. It wasn't until the twentieth century that technological breakthroughs offered the possibility of increasing yields without damaging the fertility of the land.

THE GREEN REVOLUTION[36]

The story of English wheat is typical of the pattern of development. It took almost a thousand years for wheat yields to increase from 0.5 to 2 metric tons per hectare, but only 40 years to climb from 2 to 6 metric tons per hectare.

A 1967 report of the US President's Science Advisory Committee concluded: 'The scale, severity and duration of the world food problem are so great that a massive, long-range, innovative, effort unprecedented in human history will be required to master it.'

From the mid-1960s a concerted development effort focused on spreading new techniques and scientific advances to the developing world. In 1968, William S. Gaud, administrator for the US Agency for International Development (USAID), coined the phrase 'Green Revolution' to describe this phenomenon.

The injection of aid funding and USAID's focus on the issue raised the profile of the Green Revolution and prompted the involvement of philanthropists. Both the Ford and Rockefeller foundations responded by establishing an international agricultural research system to help transfer scientific advances to developing nations. Its initial focus was on boosting the yield of rice and wheat, two of the most important crops in the developing world.

Rice production was increased through the breeding of high yield varieties (HYVs). Similar efforts were applied to wheat production, with Norman Borlaug being awarded the Nobel Peace Prize for his groundbreaking work in developing high-yielding wheat.

By 1970, about 20 percent of the wheat area and 30 percent of the rice area in developing countries were planted to HYVs, and by 1990 the share had increased to about 70 percent for both crops. These changes more than doubled cereal production in Asia between 1970 and 1995, while the population increased by 60 percent. Instead of widespread famine, cereal and calorie availability per person increased by nearly 30 percent, and wheat and rice became cheaper.

Over time, the term Green Revolution was broadened to include other major food crops such as sorghum, millet, maize, cassava, and beans. Today, a fully-fledged system of international agricultural research centers works on improving food production in the developing world.

The Green Revolution has led to increases in crop yields, raising farmers' incomes, and stimulating economic activity through a general increase in demand for goods and services in these countries. Real per capita incomes almost doubled in Asia between 1970 and 1995, and poverty fell from nearly three out of every five Asians in 1975 to less than one in five by 1995.

In India, the proportion of the rural population living below the poverty line – between 50 and 65 percent before 1965 – steadily declined to about one third by 1993. Research shows that much of this improvement can be attributed to agricultural growth and falling food prices. Other parts of the developing world, especially in Latin America, also benefited.

But the Green Revolution has been less effective elsewhere. In Sub-Saharan Africa, in particular, poor infrastructure, high transport costs, and underinvestment in irrigation, hampered progress. Moreover, critics claim that the Green Revolution has resulted in environmental damage and increased income inequality, favoring wealthier farmers with more land over smaller-scale farmers. These issues are now the focus for the next wave of development and aid.

BRINGING WATER

Another example of the power of development aid to improve lives is the use of aid in Chad to improve access to water.[37]

Chad is a landlocked country that experiences recurrent drought and inflows of refugees. Approximately 44 percent of the country's population lacks access to a supply of clean drinking water (potable water), and there are hundreds of thousands of refugees from Sudan and the Central African Republic dwelling in already vulnerable host communities.

Since 2008, the United States Agency for International Development (USAID) has partnered with Africare to carry out a development food assistance program that, among other efforts, focuses on improving access to clean drinking water. Greater water access has led to increased knowledge and demand for proper chlorination practices, resulting in the disinfection of over 11 million liters of water. Eighty one percent of program beneficiaries have adopted proper water hygiene behaviors, including hand washing and using latrines. Village residents have noticed significant positive changes, such as a decrease in water-borne diseases and reduced levels of malnutrition and child mortality rates.

Families from Mourdaba village, a small community located 45 kilometers north of Abeche, for example, report reduced cases of diarrhea since the program began. Abdelmadjid Ali, a 41-year-old father of five children, is a member of the village's water management committee. 'There was no community organization dealing with water management before the project,' he recalls. 'Villagers consumed dirty and unclean water and this exposed them to all kind of diseases including diarrhea and cholera.'[38]

To increase access to clean water in Chad, the project has constructed 113 wells since 2008 throughout Batha and Ouaddai, two of the most vulnerable, food-insecure regions. Built in mostly high population-density areas, the wells now benefit almost 35,000 people throughout the targeted regions.

Community members were directly involved in the projects, helping with some of the well construction in exchange for food through a Food-for-Work program. USAID partner Africare also brought in local experts to handle the technical aspects of well construction.

To make sure communities could manage the new potable wells and ensure proper water quality in the long term, villagers came together to create water-point management committees. Through monthly sensitization sessions, committees learned how to raise awareness about water hygiene, sanitation around water points, and purification of drinking water, including treatment of water with chlorine.

Since the start of the program, 84 villages have established functional water committees. This new method of managing water systems has been a community effort, as households contribute 20 cents each month to maintain the wells.

Village members have observed improvements in overall health since the program began. 'Since 2009, with the construction of wells in the village, training and sensitization, villagers are drinking clean water, and diseases linked to water are observed less and less in the village,' Ali notes. In fact, Ali observes that his village was spared from the 2011 outbreak of cholera and attributes this to improved water management. Water committees are now planning for the future so that they can continue disinfecting water and managing the new water system without further assistance from Africare or USAID.

AID AT WORK

These examples highlight the importance and efficacy of official aid. The so-called Green Revolution demonstrates the impact that the developed world can have when it acts in concert to transfer knowledge to the developing world, while the example of USAID's work with potable water in Chad shows how an individual country or region can gain long-term benefits from well-thought-out aid programs.

Whether it is finding new ways to feed people, improving public health, increasing access to water, or stepping in during a crisis, government-backed aid has the power to change millions of people's lives for the better. For aid efforts to have the most impact, though, governments need to keep up with the latest developments in the aid ecosystem, and seek out innovative initiatives wherever they are being practiced to address the years of inefficiency and ineffectiveness that have plagued aid programs in many places around the world.

Now, perhaps more than ever before, it is the right time to revisit and rethink aid and aid programs. The world in which aid is delivered is changing rapidly, and the nature of foreign aid is changing with it.

New donors are emerging, challenging traditional approaches to delivering aid. New models of aid provision are being introduced and existing models diversified. Donors are pursuing their own objectives through aid programs, in some ways more explicitly than ever before.

At the same time, global issues are becoming more intertwined. Responses require greater cooperation and reliance on multilateral bodies such as the United Nations, the World Bank, and other regional organizations. This is also evident in an increasing interest in building partnerships, and the specific focus on trilateral cooperation which has emerged.

The importance of cooperation in delivering effective aid was recognized in the Busan Partnership agreement, concluded at the Fourth High Level Forum on Aid Effectiveness at Busan, South Korea in November 2011, which 'sets out principles, commitments and actions that offer a foundation for effective co-operation in support of international development'.

EVOLVING AID

When people refer to 'aid', they are likely to be referring to ODA (Official Development Assistance), as defined by the Development Assistance Committee (DAC) of the OECD. However, there are also a number of new emerging aid donors that do not conform to the DAC's official definition of aid.

The modern history of official development assistance dates back to the nineteenth century, and the assistance that colonial powers provided to their colonies – in particular the British Empire and its colonies. In 1929, Britain passed the Colonial Development Act which set up a Colonial Development Advisory Committee, supervised by the British government and specifically the Secretary of State for the Colonies. Initially, it focused on infrastructure projects, primarily to improve the ability of the colonies to trade.

Another driving force in the development of official development assistance was the postscript to World War II. The drive to secure a better, safer world and economic stability in a war-torn world led to the establishment of a number of international institutions, many of which remain today.

The International Bank for Reconstruction and Development (part of the World Bank) and the International Monetary Fund (IMF) were both founded in 1944. The United Nations' Food and Agriculture Organization was launched in 1945. The Marshall Plan extended a US-backed recovery plan to Europe in 1947 and the recipients of that aid formed the Organization for European Economic Co-operation in the following year. Also, in 1948, the World Health Organization was established in Geneva. The US launched its own international aid initiative under the auspices of the Point Four program in 1949.

The foundation of the Development Assistance Committee of the OECD came in another wave of development aid initiatives in the 1960s. The OEEC set up the Development Assistance Group (DAG) in 1960 as a forum for donors to discuss assistance to developing countries. The DAG adopted a Common Aid Effort resolution in 1961, at a time when the US, UK, and France were providing the majority of official aid to developing countries. Then, after the OECD was formed in 1961, the DAG was reconstituted under the auspices of the OECD as the Development Assistance Committee (DAC).

DEFINING MOMENTS

Broadly accepted definitions of aid are elusive. That was certainly the case with the term 'official development assistance'. It took until 1972 to agree on an official definition for ODA. The definition can still be found on the OECD's website. It states that ODA is: 'provided by official agencies, including state and local governments, or by their executive agencies; and … is administered with the promotion of the economic development and welfare of developing countries as its main objective; and is concessional in character and conveys a grant element of at least 25 percent (calculated at a rate of discount of 10 percent).'[39]

Effectively, ODA is the money that wealthier nations provide to developing ones to enhance their welfare and help them grow economically. By definition, to qualify as Official Development Assistance, at least 25 percent of an aid transaction must be a grant – money that does not need to be repaid.

While the intention behind the DAC definition was clear, it has become increasingly problematic. Concessionality is defined, in part, based on a grant element of at least 25 percent at a 10 percent discount rate. In other words, to qualify as ODA, the interest rate and grace period of an official loan must make it at least 25 percent cheaper over time than a hypothetical comparison loan with no grace period and a fixed interest rate of 10 percent.

This DAC definition made a lot of sense years ago when interest rates were high. But when interest rates have fallen to less than 5 percent in many countries, it can lead to unintended situations. For example, it is easy to imagine a situation where there are official loans with a grant element of over 25 percent, but where the interest rate charged is twice that charged by commercial banks.

The DAC definition is not the only definition of aid. There are others. A number of multilateral institutions are valuable members of the aid ecosystem. These institutions include the World Bank, the International Monetary Fund (IMF), the United Nations and the United Nations Development Program (UNDP), and UNICEF.

Some of these organizations use definitions of aid that have stricter standards than the DAC definition. The IMF and World Bank use commercial interest rates as their comparison criteria and stipulate a 35 percent grant element, for example.

And, as will be discussed in more detail, there is also the impact of new donors to consider. Aid is now flowing from countries that were aid recipients not long ago. China, and some other low- and upper-middle- income countries, not members of the OECD or the DAC, provide aid via grants, concessional loans (low interest), and zero-rate loans. It is a trend *The Economist* has tagged 'Aid 2.0'.[40] Remember, too, that aid objectives do not need to be developmental. Countries may provide aid for non-altruistic reasons that further their own interests, whether that is acquiring soft power or political influence, or making economic gains.

THE 0.7 PERCENT CHALLENGE[41]

One of the biggest challenges faced by countries in need of developmental aid is that there is a finite amount of international aid available. Countries have been encouraged to give a proportion of their national wealth.

Nearly half a century ago, in 1970, wealthy countries pledged 0.7 percent of their Gross National Product (this indicator was replaced by Gross National Income in 1993) to Official Development Assistance in a United Nations General Assembly resolution.

As the OECD notes in its account of the establishment of the 0.7 percent target, this figure became the best-known international target for the amount of development aid individual countries committed to giving. The 0.7 percent target dates back to an earlier suggestion by the World Council of Churches in 1958 of a 1 percent of income target for donations to developing countries. By 1968, after various amendments including the adoption of Gross National Product as the measure of income, all the DAC members at the time signed up to the target. However, the initiative ran into difficulty. The 1 percent target included private capital flows, over which the governments of the donor countries had no control. Given that these private capital flows made up a significant proportion of the aid disbursed, 45 percent at one point, it made it difficult to determine the comparative aid burden shouldered by the donor countries.

Following work by Nobel Prize-winning economist Jan Tinbergen, who led the United Nations Committee on Development Planning, a target of 0.75 percent of GNP was proposed, for both concessional and non-concessional official flows. Negotiations between developed and developing countries continued until a figure of 0.7 percent was agreed on. In October 1970, a UN General Assembly Resolution stated: 'Each economically advanced country will progressively increase its official development assistance to the developing countries and will exert its best efforts to reach a minimum net amount of 0.7 percent of its Gross National Product at market prices by the middle of the decade.'

Most DAC members signed up to the 0.7 percent target. There were some countries that preferred not to. These included the US, which did not want to commit to specific targets. Other countries, such as Switzerland, were not members of the UN.

Sweden, the Netherlands, Norway, and Denmark all hit the target by 1978, and continued to do so consistently. Finland and Luxembourg have also hit the target, but the other DAC members have yet to reach it and, according to the latest figures, the weighted average for the ODA for DAC member has yet to pass 0.4 percent of GNP.

Despite mixed success on achieving the 0.7 percent target it remains the standard for many countries and has been referenced in a number of important aid and development conferences and agreements. In 2012, for example, members of the European Union reaffirmed their commitment to increase collective aid spending to 0.7 percent of GNI by 2015, at the same time as reaffirming all ODA commitments made individually and collectively, and it also formed part of the Millennium Development Goals.

2
The rise of the new donors

Broadly speaking, there are two philosophical approaches to aid which shape the practical approach to developing an aid strategy and program. These are, first, assistance-driven aid; and second, investment-driven aid – though to a large extent aid allocation can be a combination of both.

Developed countries – notably the 28 members of the OECD's Development Assistance Committee, including the US, the UK, France, and the EU as a whole – typically follow what might be termed the assistance-driven aid approach, providing funds that are, in the main, untied to any particular economic outcome. They are focused instead on improving conditions in social sectors, such as health and education, while also contributing assistance for improving infrastructure and boosting agricultural and manufacturing production, as well as direct support of government budgets, in some cases.

The larger donor countries usually mix their developmental motives with geopolitical goals, such as establishing better relations with certain countries, trying to influence their governance models, or attempting to obtain economic benefits. Others, most notably the Nordic countries, often provide more tightly focused aid unconnected, at least explicitly, to such outcomes.

From an operational standpoint, it is argued that the great advantage of the assistance-driven model (although this is disputed by some) lies in the apparent 'transparency of the process' for deciding who gets aid, and the flexibility it gives recipient countries to use some of the aid as they see fit. Most such programs operate through clear processes and guidelines, with clearly stated goals which often include the transfer of knowledge to the recipients as well as money.

On the other hand, the conditional nature of the assistance approach often leads to a relatively rigid development model that can fail to recognize other, more diversified ways to provide aid or to create synergies between the public and private spheres. And because many such programs require recipients to maintain a certain level of governance, donors often face the dilemma that very few countries actually satisfy those standards.

An alternative approach is investment-driven aid. The goals of countries following the investment-driven model are typically more straightforward: to gain an economic benefit (with a real business case) by investing in the development and export of natural resources, while also aiding the country invested in. This typically takes the form of loans made directly to countries in a region to support large infrastructure and agricultural projects and smaller development projects, such as schools, often through the originating country's export-import bank. While the relationship and quid pro quo between countries is not always transparent, the donor usually manages to secure some kind of gain, such as economic concessions in the form of access to natural resources and trade.

China exemplifies this strategy. Its hybrid approach combines export credits to subsidize exports, and natural-resources-backed lines of credit to finance projects primarily in economic infrastructure, energy and resource development, and industry, while retaining control of the projects' construction and management. Both India and Brazil are also increasing their investment-driven aid, including a greater use of loans from their own export-import banks. In both cases, however, their motives tend to be less economic and more humanitarian and development-oriented in comparison to the Chinese.

Investment-driven aid, when conducted well, can encourage resource-rich African countries to reinvest at least part of the revenues into other, wider, national development efforts. Moreover, these deals create a strong incentive for investor countries to complete projects successfully, since they shoulder the financial risk.

However, these deals can create several risks for recipient economies. For example, the strategy can lead to the fragmentation of aid unless recipient countries can link the projects together into an overall strategy for how foreign investment can best promote development throughout the country's economy. (This is discussed later.)

THE CHANGING LANDSCAPE

Prior to the financial crisis of 2008 and the recession that followed, many countries already fell short of their commitment to contribute 0.7 percent of their GNIs to Official Development Assistance. Worldwide, Official Development Assistance was about $112 billion in 2008, and originated primarily from the 28 countries in the Development Assistance Committee.

As of 2008, the cumulative shortfall in aid contributions vis-à-vis the 1970 target was almost $4 trillion. The existing data on the link between Gross National Income and the level of aid a country provides suggests that the shortfall is likely to grow – at least in the short term, post-financial crisis. The data reveals that there is a correlation between GNI and the level of aid, and that there is a delay of about five years before changes in GNI feed through to the amount of aid donated.

Traditional Western donors may have reduced flexibility as a result of economic and financial challenges at home. In turn this may impact their level of international giving and place even more emphasis on contributions from new and emerging donors.

Even so, in 2013 development aid rose by 6.1 percent in real terms to reach the highest level ever recorded, while in 2014 development aid flows were stable.[42] Donors provided a total of $135.2 billion in net ODA in 2014, marginally up from the $135.1 billion the year before. But this represented a 0.5 percent decline in real terms.

A number of governments stepped up their spending on foreign aid, with 13 out of 28 countries increasing their donations in 2014. The rise followed an increase in 2013 after two years of falling volumes. However, it is possible that the full impact of the financial crisis may not have yet fed through to aid budgets. The GNI shock that many Development Assistance Committee countries experienced following 2008, and in some cases are continuing to experience, may yet lead to an extended fall in in aid contributions. Notably, 15 countries reduced ODA in 2014.

Certainly the five top DAC donors may be particularly hard-pressed to maintain their previous levels of aid contribution, when a combination of economic strategies designed to prime growth, including bailouts and stimulus from expansionary monetary policy, have caused budget deficits to soar.

Despite the rise in giving in 2014 the underfunding of aid pledges may well continue, exacerbating the aid shortfall for certain countries. There is pressure in some countries for aid to be curtailed severely. And, while some countries will continue to fulfill their aid pledges, in the short to medium term international aid is likely to suffer. The ODA challenge for the least-developed countries is highlighted by the reduction in bilateral aid to these countries in 2014 of 16 percent in real terms.

THE NEW DONORS

Attitudes towards which countries should be recipients of aid are changing, as are the countries donating aid. Previous recipient countries are now emerging as new donors. Many of these countries have been providing aid for some time but their donations are now sizeable. As a result competing models of aid are emerging, and putting pressure on traditional donors to improve their performance.

For many years the list of the major development aid donors was dominated by the developed nations. But the network of ODA donors is changing. Since the 1960s, the percentage of aid donated by the Development Assistance Committee's five largest donors has been steadily declining, decade on decade, from 87 percent to roughly 62 percent.

While DAC members still account for the overwhelming majority of ODA, the amount contributed by other nations is increasing. There are more than twice as many donor countries today as there were in the 1960s. Globalization and the rise in economic power of many developing countries, coupled with the economic problems besetting some of the biggest donor countries, have created an opportunity for new leaders to emerge in the area of international aid.

South Korea was among the first to do so and has since become a DAC country. Not all emerging donors wish to become part of the DAC, however; many prefer to set their own aid rules. Perhaps the most obvious example is China. In 2007, for the first time, the value of foreign assistance disbursed by China exceeded the amount that it received in ODA. Since then the gap between the country's aid outflows and inflows has increased as China assumes an increasingly important role as an aid donor. China has become an important provider of aid to its Asian neighbors and has become increasingly sophisticated about using tied aid in Africa, where it has loan agreements with over 20 countries. For example, Angola guarantees China access to 10,000 barrels of oil a day in return for a $2 billion concessionary loan.

China is not alone. Other BRIC countries, such as Brazil and India, have also become donors of development aid, as have some countries in the Middle East, notably GCC countries such as Saudi Arabia, UAE, Kuwait, and Qatar.

Historically, Arab countries, led by Saudi Arabia, have been generous providers of ODA, especially when the price of oil has been strong. Arab ODA was particularly high in the 1970s and early 1980s, reaching 12 percent of gross national incomes in the UAE and about 8 percent in Saudi Arabia and Kuwait.[43] In 2013, the UAE had the highest aid to GNI ratio in the world. Most DAC countries contributed about 0.3 percent of their gross national incomes to ODA between 1973 and 2008, while Arab countries averaged 1.5 percent. That was five times the DAC average and more than twice the United Nations target.

Arab ODA has been the equivalent of about 13 percent of total DAC ODA in recent years. In addition, Arab donors have followed the practice of pooling some of their aid money, and many regional banks, such as the Islamic Development Bank, also provide multilateral aid based on donations from regional countries. Furthermore, Arab donors have branched out from their Arab League focus, and now make significant aid contributions to other parts of the world such as Africa and South Asia.

The progress the Gulf countries are making as aid donors is evident from the UAE becoming a DAC participant in July 2014. Participant status allows the UAE to take part in non-confidential Committee meetings, including high-level and senior-level meetings, and meetings of the DAC subsidiary bodies.

While it is not allowed to participate in formal decision-making processes, participant status allows the UAE to contribute to the international development debate, and learn from the aid experiences of other DAC members.

DIVERGENT APPROACHES

The growing diversity of aid donors has been accompanied by an increase in the variety of approaches taken and models adopted.

Despite their high level of giving, Arab countries remain relatively informal in their approach to aid. For instance, Arab donors typically do not state their objectives or document the overarching purposes of their ODA. For the most part, they have not formalized their internal governance models to manage their aid. Also, Arab donors are not, for the most part, very rigorous about the way in which they measure their aid results, in many cases allowing the implementing agencies to gauge their own success and make their own adjustments. It is comparatively recently that these increasingly influential aid donors have begun to think through the new imperative of development effectiveness.

It is also very difficult to gauge the overall amount of aid donated by Arab countries and, as a result, much of the aid from Arab donors gets little attention globally. Take interventions during the 2015 Syrian crisis. Since many of the GCC donors do not provide aid through UN agencies, or through a particular agency, the media has incorrectly assumed that the total aid contribution from GCC countries is low. But, in reality, they have been among the most generous donors. The fragmented and less publicized nature of their aid means that GCC countries need to build soft power and build awareness of their aid program contributions.

Some of the same challenges are evident among BRIC donors, most of which are also still ODA recipients. Like Arab donors, BRIC donors tend not to have organized governance or evaluation systems for their ODA. There are some exceptions. Russia is more advanced in terms of aid evaluation as it has established a dedicated aid agency, the Russian Agency for International Development. India has a similar body, the Indian Agency for Partnership in Development. Both Brazil and China are considering forming independent aid agencies, but are at an earlier stage in the process.

There are both altruistic and self-interested aspects to the aid emanating from the BRIC countries, just as there is with aid originating in the Western or Arab worlds. China and India are good examples of aid that is often self-interested. Take, for example, the intense focus that the aid programs of both countries have on Africa, a continent rich in energy and other natural resources.

Indeed, most of China's aid is believed to be tied. This may be in the form of Chinese firms being awarded contracts to build projects in recipient countries, often supplying their own Chinese workforce. As a result, many of the benefits arising from these contracts go to Chinese firms. They may also provide loans or assistance repaid in oil by energy-rich African countries such as Angola, Nigeria, Ethiopia, and Sudan. In contrast, only 25 percent of Russia's aid, much of which is directed to former Soviet Union countries, is made with the same kind of obligations or expectations.

In recent years, the BRIC countries have put more of their focus on triangular cooperation, whether of the North-South-South or of South-South-South variety. An example of the North-South-South arrangement is Brazil's work with Northern donors and multilateral agencies to provide health-related aid to Portuguese-speaking countries in Africa, Latin America, and elsewhere. The India-Brazil-South Africa Fund for Poverty Alleviation created in 2003, is an example of a South-South-South triangular arrangement. (See page 56 for more details on triangular arrangements.)

THE CHINESE WAY

China is the most obvious example of how new donors are changing perspectives about the way aid works.

The standardized definition of ODA for DAC members is precise: official financing, concessional in character and promoting the economic development and welfare of developing countries. The grant element has to be at least 25 percent, the discount rate 10 percent. Export credit-agency lending solely for promoting exports is excluded, as is funding destined for firms from the donor country, intended to boost their private investment in the recipient country. The cost to the donor is important, too, under the DAC definition. If a donor was providing a loan at market rate plus a margin, for example, this would not count as ODA. Nor does military aid qualify.

The DAC also specified a category of financial flows directed towards foreign assistance, 'other official flows', that does not conform to the ODA's definition. The use of export credits alone or alongside is governed by the OECD's Export Credit Group.

China's approach to aid is markedly different to the more traditional approach associated with the DAC. Deborah Bräutigam, Professor of International Political Economy and Director of the International Development Program (IDEV) at Johns Hopkins University's School of Advanced International Studies (SAIS) in Washington, illustrated some of the differences in a paper in *The Journal of International Development*. She noted that 'China's official aid program is non-transparent and poorly understood'.[44]

China's external assistance includes zero interest and concessional loans. Aid grants and loans are administered by the Ministry of Commerce, indicative of their approach to aid, and support China's diplomatic objectives. A 1998 Ministry of Finance document revealed some items in the aid budget. These included the costs of military goods, rebates for certain expenses incurred by Chinese firms involved in foreign aid-financed joint investment and cooperation projects, and fees and expenses for firms administering aid projects. Funding from other budgets support subsidized export credits, and provides incentives for Chinese firms to develop trade zones overseas.

The China Development Bank provides equity investment to African countries through its China Africa Development Fund. China Eximbank offers credits for buyers of its exports and suppliers via Chinese firms. China's official loan finance tends to be at commercial rates plus a margin.

China has created aid projects that, while having the appearance of ODA, are financed by non-ODA means. As Bräutigam mentions in her paper (and her book *The Dragon's Gift*), China provided Angola with special state loans, a renewable credit line which ran to $10 billion between 2003 and 2010, directed towards a range of Angolan post-war infrastructure development projects covering education, industry, agriculture, healthcare, roads and transport, and energy networks. The loans were made against oil exports, and on better terms (but still commercial) both structurally and regarding interest rates, than alternative loans available at the time.

Cooperation between China and OECD countries on aid is theoretically possible, albeit with barriers to overcome. There are commonalities in the way the DAC and China provide foreign assistance, including the way they construct projects, provide technical assistance, humanitarian assistance, and debt relief, for example. And, as Bräutigam again highlights, there is some overlap between the principles governing Chinese foreign aid and the Paris Declaration norms.

However, while the OECD countries have agreed not to tie aid, and to untie aid where necessary, China's aid principles explicitly endorse the use of Chinese-manufactured equipment, and often favor Chinese firms. DAC aid is often directed at the improvement of specific aspect of the recipient country's policy and comes with economic and political conditions attached. China is, perhaps, more interested in the economic benefits it obtains than attempting to change the country in receipt of its assistance. Another major barrier to cooperation between China and the DAC members is that China is not, and is unlikely to become, a member of the DAC.

3
Does aid work?

Providing aid is challenging. After all, as critics argue, widespread poverty still persists in many parts of the world – such as the Democratic Republic of Congo, New Guinea, and Somalia among others – despite high flows of aid.

There are many obstacles that can prevent aid from reaching the recipients who need assistance the most, the poorest and most disadvantaged. Corruption is one barrier. When large multi-million dollar projects are being implemented in countries with poor governance structures, there is significant scope for funds being misplaced. Insufficient targeting of aid programs can also mean that funds fail to reach the intended recipients. Fragmentation of aid is another barrier, where a lack of coherent and coordinated aid strategy and delivery mechanisms lessens the eventual impact.

Even when it is carefully targeted, aid is not always effective. For example, humanitarian aid tends to flow toward nations with high poverty levels, such as Palestine, Liberia, Chad, and Zimbabwe, yet the poverty rate remains persistently high at about 80 percent.

It is not clear how much, if any, of that aid reaches the people who need it the most: the people who are starving, ill, or displaced from their homes. Haiti, for example, received a significant amount of aid prior to the earthquake in 2010. Yet despite this aid effort poverty persisted in Haiti, exacerbating the impact of the earthquake.

Likewise, aid aimed at debt relief often fails to reach the countries it is intended for. In 2007, for example, Indonesia, Kenya, and Honduras had external debt equivalent to more than a quarter of their GDP. But, despite the level of indebtedness, each country received less than $50 million in debt relief.

Tied aid is another potential source of ineffectiveness and inequity. Aid may be provided on condition that the recipient uses goods and services from donor countries. These goods and services, however, may be overpriced. The amounts provided in aid may be dwarfed by the benefits obtained by donor countries through protectionism. Wealthier countries may deny market access to the products of poorer countries, while at the same time using aid as a lever to open the markets in those same poorer countries to their products. If the donor country uses its own citizens as employees to run its projects it may also hamper the development of human capital, an educated and productive workforce, in the recipient country.

AID INTERVENTIONS – INVALUABLE OR INEFFECTIVE?

There are different schools of thought on the usefulness of ODA. A libertarian approach, for example, objects to the heavy hand of government providing, planning, and implementing aid projects. Critics such as economists Peter Bauer and Milton Friedman, both influential libertarians, have criticized state aid on the grounds that it has led to enlarged government bureaucracies, perpetuated bad governments, enriched the elite in poor countries, or just been wasted.

Among the critics is William Easterly, an American economist, professor of economics at New York University and author of *The White Man's Burden: Why the West's Efforts to Aid the Rest Have Done So Much Ill and So Little Good*. Easterly argues that aid interventions directed at improving education, or forgiving debt, for example, have failed to achieve their intended objectives in many cases. Governments need to learn how to incentivize growth, and prompt individuals to invest in their own future.

Some critics argue for a complete reform of aid. Others suggest that aid has supported poverty reduction and growth in some countries and prevented worsening poverty in others.

Supporters of aid counter that many of the critics' arguments are overstated. While aid may fail sometimes, some aid is better than no aid. The American economist Jeffery Sachs is an advocate of aid as part of a package of measures designed to eradicate poverty and promote growth.

Much aid today is aimed at solving what have been called the 'wicked problems' of our age. The origins of the term can be traced to work by the design theorists Horst Rittel and Melvin Webber. In the 1970s they developed their idea of wicked problems in a social policy planning context. The problems defied solution through rational scientific problem-solving methods.

Today 'wicked problems' has become a phrase that is commonly applied to issues such as climate change, healthcare, crime, and social injustice. Many of these wicked problems involve issues that aid is attempting to address.

Frequently, these problems are global in nature, and as such an effective response requires cooperation on a supra-national scale. Climate change is just one example. Without globally concerted policy measures, the trajectory of global greenhouse gas emissions poses significant threats to economic development and environmental sustainability. Moving to a sustainable path requires global cooperation.

We can expect the desire and need to solve wicked problems, such as dealing with climate change, and the need to cooperate globally in order to do so, to drive even more effective aid cooperation.

MAKING AID COUNT

Given the mixed picture on aid efficiency, differing assessments from economists on the usefulness or otherwise of aid, with many of the major donors under pressure to reduce ODA donations, and the challenges that societies face becoming more complex and numerous, it is increasingly important to make sure that any aid given is as effective as possible. Aid effectiveness is key to achieving developmental outcomes. This is a major challenge for donor countries.

Countries are thinking more broadly about aid. They are moving beyond the narrower focus on aid effectiveness to encompass a more comprehensive concept of development effectiveness. They realize the aid that they provide needs to work within a broader foreign policy context that covers trade, finance, security, immigration, and drug enforcement, for example.

Donor countries are also more likely to earmark their aid for a specific purpose within a target country. Social infrastructure and services – like schools and healthcare – are the biggest sector focus, followed by debt relief. As a result the portion of aid money that the recipient country can use in any way it wishes has shriveled to 2 percent, down from 22 percent in the 1970s.

Growth in the number of donors is good news for recipients but it has a downside, as it has made the aid landscape more complex and fragmented. Recipient countries often have multiple donors, and more than half of those donors typically change their allocations from year to year.

In the changing aid landscape, there is room for the donor and recipient to consider more optimal models of aid together. The emerging donors are not necessarily new to ODA; many of them have been giving for years. But as they start accounting for a bigger percentage of global contributions, these emerging donors have an opportunity to forge effective ODA strategies and adopt more rigorous aid management practices.

4
Towards an aid strategy

With the shifting ODA landscape, the growth in the numbers of donors, the changing ODA roles of countries, and the pressure to think more broadly about development effectiveness, ODA strategy is more important than ever.

Having an aid strategy is not just important for aid that falls within DAC definitions. It is important because an aid strategy, whether altruistic or not, is likely to yield better benefits for everyone. It will allow for better measurement of outcomes, improve the outcome for recipients, increase the benefits to the donor (be it soft capital or financial return) and is likely to ration resources in a much better way.

This does not just mean strategy from an isolated country perspective. Today, there is a complex network of players involved in delivering aid and developmental goals effectively. Any strategy must take account of this network.

At any point in time, one country within the ODA ecosystem may well be providing aid to a number of different countries. At the same time other countries in the ODA ecosystem will also be providing aid to multiple recipient countries. From the perspective of the recipient country, there will be multiple donors providing aid.

For most donors there are two types of driver behind the provision of aid. There is the provision of aid from an altruistic perspective, providing aid because the donor wants to develop the country that they are providing aid to. At the same time, and more importantly from the donor country's perspective, there may be selfish motives at work as the donor is trying to meet its own geopolitical and economic goals by donating that aid.

JOINING THE DOTS

Potentially, each donor will have its own aid objectives and these objectives are likely to cut across each other. Given this tangled network of donors without harmonization and communication of strategies across the members of the ODA ecosystem, donors-to-donors and donors-to-recipients, aid is likely to be fragmented and far less effective than it could be otherwise.

There are already some mechanisms for the harmonization of aid. The OECD's Development Assistance Committee (DAC) is a good example of this. In 2003, the OECD produced a 124-page report devoted to DAC member harmonization on aid delivery.[45] The report was the product of work by the DAC, which set up a special task force to investigate the simplification and harmonization of aid donor procedures. It covered a range of project-related activities, including country analysis and project preparation, reporting and monitoring, financial aspects, and delegated cooperation. The DAC has guidelines on reporting where aid is flowing to, for example, and there is also a system of peer review of member donations in order to try and increase the alignment of aid objectives.

The 2008 OECD report 'Effective Aid Management: Twelve lessons from DAC peer reviews' is a good example of how DAC peer reviews are used to improve the effectiveness of aid.[46] The report draws together lessons concerning aid donor strategy, and organizational management and delivery (many of these lessons can be found in this book in one form or another).

The rise of major new donors has added to the harmonization challenge. China is a good example. It is not a member of the DAC, and as an economically powerful donor it is able to pursue its own development agenda without consulting or aligning with other donors if it chooses.

This is where developing and outlining a coherent development strategy adopting current best practice becomes particularly useful. When a country is clear about its development objectives, on its capabilities and resources, where it will donate, why, and in what way, it makes harmonization easier. It also makes for more effective aid giving.

For the smaller donors, too, a well thought out strategy is particularly important. The smaller donors may find that their lack of size and economic and political power makes the effective provision of aid more difficult.

ELEMENTS OF AN AID STRATEGY

There is no surefire route to successful ODA. Nor is there a template that every country, donor, or recipient, can adopt. There are, however, a number of pillars which form parts of an efficient ODA management strategy. There are some clearly identifiable elements, and key decision points that need to be addressed, in order to develop a viable ODA.

Aid strategies depend on four building blocks. Countries must:

- First figure out what they hope to accomplish – the purpose, or drivers, of their aid programs;
- Second, donor countries need to settle on a management approach – what forms of institutional governance they will use;
- Third, they need to decide how they will allocate their available aid – the channels they will employ, and whether they will emphasize bilateral or multilateral donations;
- Fourth, they need to establish monitoring and evaluation mechanisms to assess the quality of their aid programs.

The purpose of aid

One of the first things that countries should do as they begin to develop their aid strategy is to decide what they hope to accomplish through their aid programs. What is the purpose of providing aid and what are the drivers?

Some countries have very clearly stated aid objectives. The UK, for example, focuses on the Millennium Development Goals; Denmark, via the development aid agency Danida, targets four areas: human rights and democracy, green growth, social progress, and stability and protection.

Most aid can be classified under one of three different overarching objectives: development, humanitarian, and geopolitical. Often, a donor country's aid strategy will reflect a mix of these objectives, with each donor's approach having a slightly different weighting and emphasis between the three types.

Developmental

A donor country's aid objectives may be developmental. This is where the aid is being targeted at helping the recipient country rebuild and improve its economic, social, or environmental infrastructures. Of the three main objectives, developmental aid is the broadest in terms of its possible targets and the different ways that it can be implemented in the recipient country. Its goals, for example, might include improving the economy, providing net debt relief in the recipient country, and supporting critical social services across a variety of sectors, such as education and healthcare. Poverty reduction, a push towards a United Nations Millennium Development Goal like gender equality, or assisting in the provision of potable water – these are all examples of development aid.

The exact emphasis of the development aid will depend on the circumstances of the recipient country. A country that has just emerged from a conflict, whether that is civil or cross border, and where there may be regime change, is likely to get aid in the form of full debt relief, possibly through grants. The economy of a country in this situation may need reconstruction at even the most basic level of infrastructure and market mechanisms. It may need to have its network of social institutions – such as schools and hospitals, for example – restarted and rebuilt.

Developmental aid may be just as important for countries that are more stable and have their basic infrastructure in place. In these cases aid will generally address later-stage needs, such as education or the promotion of market-based economic reforms.

While developmental aid is often considered to be at least partly altruistic in nature, it does not have to be. China is an example of developmental aid where the donor country's interests are a prime consideration in providing the aid. Although donating money for building infrastructure in African countries, for example, China benefits economically through sending Chinese companies to build those infrastructure projects, as well as through agreements for the provision of resources to China from the African recipients of aid.

Humanitarian

Another possible objective of an aid strategy is to address a recipient country's humanitarian problems, to attempt to save people's lives or to alleviate suffering.

Humanitarian aid is almost invariably provided as a response to a crisis or emergency, as disaster relief, for example. This might be after natural disasters, such as an earthquake or a tsunami – as in the case of the devastating earthquake in Haiti in 2010 or the Indian Ocean earthquake and tsunami in 2004. It might be after a man-made crisis, such as a response to an outbreak of conflict or war – take the cases of the genocide in Rwanda in 1994, for example, the Kosovo War of 1998 to 1999 and the Balkans Conflict more generally, and the refugee crisis following the recent conflict in Syria. Famine is another common reason for humanitarian intervention, such as the East African Drought in 2011, as are outbreaks of disease and illness, as seen with the global response to the outbreak of the Ebola virus in West Africa in 2014.

Due to the nature of the challenge faced when dealing with a crisis or emergency, the main humanitarian aid effort may be relatively short term in nature, with aid tailing off once the initial crisis has passed. Typically, it is obvious why the aid is being sent; politically, the decision to send humanitarian aid often has cross-party support in donor countries.

Because humanitarian aid is a quick response to a particular event, it tends to be reactive in nature. However, there is a trend towards donor countries trying to be more proactive with humanitarian aid. The focus now is on building the preparedness of countries that are prone to humanitarian crises. It is possible, for example, to identify areas of the world where there is significant risk of a natural disaster, such as an earthquake zone, or regions where there are sporadic outbreaks of a particular disease, such as hemorrhagic fever in Africa.

In these and other cases, where the risk of an event is more easily identifiable, donor and recipient countries are trying to build resilience by developing a pre-emptive response – building stockpiles of foods or medicines, for example, and creating early monitoring and detection systems.

Geopolitical

A third category of aid objectives is decidedly not altruistic. This objective involves securing some geopolitical advantage for the donor country. The aid is used to produce an outcome that will benefit the donor itself. This objective tends to be less transparent than the humanitarian and developmental ones, and is often not stated explicitly. Close examination of what the aid is being used for and the benefits accruing to the donor is usually revealing.

Geopolitical aid can be directed at a number of different targets. Once again, this usually depends on the circumstances of the recipient country. For instance, in countries recovering from war, geopolitical aid is usually intended to prevent state failure and reduce violent conflict. Or in countries that are in the process of making reforms, geopolitical aid may be used to prevent the acquisition of weapons of mass destruction, or to make sure that the country doesn't become a haven for terrorists or narcotics trafficking.

Finally, some countries use geopolitical aid to build or support partnerships with countries that they consider critical to their economic wellbeing or homeland security. This might be, for example, because of a resource that the recipient country has or because of its geographic location. An example of self-interested geopolitical aid is US funding in Iraq, Afghanistan, and Pakistan.

Since the end of the Cold War, international relations between rich and poor countries have been dominated by large flows of foreign aid as well as by the resumption of military interventions, most of them led by the US.

Concurrently, transnational terrorism has become a dominant concern for the West, especially after the events of September 2001. Hence, the 'War on Terror' dominated international relations in the wake of 9/11.

In early April 2009, President Obama asked congress for $83 billion of additional funding for Iraq and Afghanistan, intending to eradicate the Al Qaeda threat. This budget included $1.6 billion and $1.4 billion for Afghanistan and Iraq, respectively, for 'diplomatic programs and development aid'. An additional $800 million was asked for the Palestinian Authority, including some humanitarian aid for Gaza. A further $1 billion of unconditional aid to Pakistan was announced about a week later, as a provisional measure before Congress voted a $1.5-billion aid flow to this country for the next five years.

Some types of assistance, such as military support which, while they might appear to be aid, for example, do not count as Official Development Assistance contributions, according to the Organization for Economic Co-operation and Development. These include military applications of nuclear energy and nuclear nonproliferation activities; the supply of military equipment and services and the forgiveness of debt incurred for military purposes; money given to refugees after they have been in a donor country for a year (for the first 12 months, such assistance does qualify as ODA, as does the cost of repatriation); cultural programs in developing countries whose main purpose is to promote the culture or values of the donor; and activities combating terrorism and expenditures on paramilitary functions, such as counterinsurgency work and intelligence gathering.

The objectives are the overall umbrella that determines the direction of the donor's aid. Beyond that, however, the donors have to consider more specific details. Which countries, regions, sectors, projects, and themes do they want to pursue?

The size of the donor will affect the strategy employed. The aid decisions of smaller donor countries are influenced by their resource constraints. So a smaller donor, such as one of the Nordic countries, may prefer to be more focused in its country selection in order not to dilute its aid and the ability of that aid to have a lasting impact.

Although recent financial turmoil may impact Greece's ODA decisions, previously it focused Hellenic Aid on 20 priority countries clustered around the Balkans, Black Sea, and Baltic Sea regions, as well as some African and Asian countries. Aid was distributed through an annual call-for-proposals process, but there were no predefined allocation criteria as such.

Smaller countries are also likely to have a smaller number of sector focuses than large donors. Think back to Danida's four-pronged focus. Depending on their situations, smaller donors may factor in a prospect's development needs, natural resources, or national security status in deciding how to allocate their financial aid.

DAC donors direct about 30 percent of their aid on average towards a priority sector or theme. In doing so, their foreign aid strategies reflect a mix of altruism, targeting issues such as poverty reduction and educational infrastructure development, and self-interest.

Examples of altruistic ODA on the part of DAC countries include Canada's creation of a mobile hospital in Haiti and Japan's support of infectious disease prevention in places like Vietnam. On the other hand, Denmark's ODA in support of energy efficiency and environmental protection is an example of not purely altruistic aid. The country's international aid in this area is intended to promote policies that could bolster the use of wind turbines and other clean technologies, which are important to Denmark's economy. Although such technologies are likely to have great developmental impact, the motivation is not necessarily driven by pure altruism but rather by a mix of economic benefits and the competitive advantage Denmark has. Of course, there are many other aid themes that donor countries might choose to focus on. They could concentrate on empowering women, improving food security, reducing poverty, or eradicating malaria.

Another factor that donors take into account when deciding on their aid distribution strategy is to choose recipient countries for cultural reasons. There may be linguistic or political ties, geographical or colonial connections. Examples include Australia and Japan's aid contributions in Indonesia, as well as the UK's aid to its former colony India.

Management approach

The second pillar of an aid strategy is the management approach. As well as deciding on their overall aid objectives, a donor country must decide on the way in which it will manage its aid program, and the forms of institutional governance that will be used. I have identified four areas that are relevant with respect to governance. These are internal governance; collaboration and international cooperation; implementation; and financing.

Internal governance

There are two main elements, accountability and management.

The first concerns the level of accountability and enforceability a government wants to allow its aid program. A donor country can decide on a stricter form of internal governance by enshrining its aid program in legislation. This means spelling out the details of aid provision, including aid targets, and introducing accountability to government for those measures laid down in law. An alternative is to adopt a slightly more flexible solution using policies to shape its aid programs.

Both approaches have advantages and disadvantages. The important thing is that a country incorporates its aid objectives into legislation, policy, or both. Doing so demonstrates that the donor country is strongly committed to its aid strategy, whether it is through policy or legislation, thus elevating the discussion on aid to a higher level.

The DAC countries manage aid through a combination of legislation and policy statements, in which case legislation has an overriding authority, or through policy statements alone. For example, DAC countries that use both legislation and policy to manage aid include Portugal, Italy, Greece, Belgium, Austria, Luxembourg, Switzerland, the UK, the US, Denmark, Canada, and Spain.[47] DAC countries that only have policy statements governing their development cooperation include Japan, Australia, Norway, Sweden, Finland, Germany, Netherlands, New Zealand, and France.[48]

The legislative approach has the advantage of setting out the responsibilities of all the government entities involved, and of establishing their accountability. It can also protect the aid program from competing interests that get in the way of its long-term development objective.

Aid legislation, for the countries that have it, generally addresses several points. To begin with, it almost always spells out the purpose and focus areas of ODA. It may also break down the role of a lead entity responsible for the country's aid program. It may discuss how collaborations should work and, in the case of collaboration, who has the responsibility for performance oversight and evaluation.

There will probably be some targets and metrics indicated in the legislation. So, for example, there may be a numerical target for the percentage of gross national income that the country should devote to ODA. It is worth noting that while setting targets and metrics shows commitment from government it can also prove restrictive. Numerical targets are important, but they do not reflect the nature of aid and its ability to change lives. They may encourage too much focus on the numbers rather than the outcomes that are possible. They may, unnecessarily, limit our perception of what is possible through aid.

Countries that have a strong legislative component to their aid programs include the UK, with its International Development Act, and Canada, with its ODA Accountability Act. Both clearly lay out mandates for their countries' ODA efforts, identify goals and objectives, and prescribe mechanisms of oversight and evaluation. There are also some disadvantages to embedding an aid program into a legislative framework. It can hinder efficiency, for instance, especially over the long run if laws are not updated regularly. It can also obstruct measures aimed at harmonizing aid initiatives, such as those called for in the 2005 Paris Declaration and the 2008 Accra Agenda for Action.

Countries that use policies and policy statements to outline their aid strategy generally obtain more flexibility with respect to adapting to those issues requiring cross-country cooperation.

In addition, policy statements may work better than legislation in establishing a common purpose in countries that have several entities administering their foreign assistance, and may give civil society organizations – critical in aid implementation – an important say in the development of aid programs.

While they lack the same legislative force, policy statements are still able to cover some of the same ground as legislation. They could, for example, stipulate that multilateral aid should not exceed a certain percentage of total aid, or specify that a donor country should meet the UN target for wealthy countries, which is to allocate 0.7 percent of their gross national product to ODA. Examples of aid-related policy statements include 'An Effective Aid Program for Australia,' Norway's 'Fighting Poverty Together,' and the Netherlands' Ministry of Affairs' 'Our Common Concern.'

The second element of internal governance concerns the way that the donor country sets up its system for managing its aid program. With the DAC countries, the ministry of foreign affairs or its equivalent always bears the ultimate responsibility for implementing aid programs. Beyond that, four basic governance models have emerged in DAC countries.

First comes complete centralization. In some countries a standalone agency is given the responsibility for running the country's aid program, both in terms of policy and implementation. A good example of this is where the Department for International Development (DFID) in the UK has been headed by the Secretary of State for International Development, with the goal 'to promote sustainable development and eliminate world poverty.'

Next is partial centralization. Some big aid donors, such as the US, Germany, and France, have followed this model. In partial centralization the ministry of foreign affairs takes overall responsibility for policy, and a separate agency is responsible for delivering on policy and handling aid implementation. In turn, this agency reports to and is accountable to the ministry.

A third possible model is to make aid or development its own agency residing within the ministry of foreign affairs or its equivalent – effectively organized by purpose of aid. In this case, the agency makes decisions based on aid objectives. The countries that have adopted models similar to this include Switzerland and the Netherlands.

The final model is of aid organized around recipient countries. Some donor countries have foreign affairs ministries that are organized along regional lines. So there might be an Africa department, an Asia Department, and so on. These countries are able to adopt an aid governance model that allows the regional departments to manage aid to the countries on which they already work. Countries that have used this type of system include Denmark and Norway.

Whether a country decides to set up a dedicated body reporting to the minister of foreign affairs, to align governance to aid objectives, or separate its aid management out on a regional basis, will depend on the structure of the government. There is no right or wrong approach, per se.

Indeed, the approach to managing aid is likely to change, often with changes in government. Canada used to operate a centralized standalone agency, the Canadian International Development Agency (CIDA), founded in 1968, which dealt with Canada's foreign aid programs. However, in March 2013, the Conservative government said that it would be incorporating CIDA into the Department of Foreign Affairs, renaming the combined organization the Department of Foreign Affairs, Trade and Development.

The four models outlined above reflect the current trend in aid governance with new donor countries, such as India, Brazil, and to some extent Russia, setting up aid programs in keeping with these models.

There are, however, outliers. China is evolving a new model where its aid donation is mostly centered in its export banks with overall strategy handled within the Ministry of Commerce. This is a reflection of the very different nature of China's aid approach, which is primarily economically driven.

Collaboration and international cooperation

The traditional model for international aid cooperation, which has defined the ODA landscape until recently, involved countries in the developed North providing aid and assistance to developing countries in the South. More recently the international aid paradigm has extended to include South-South cooperation, usually between the more developed BRIC countries, for example, and other developing nations in the south.

The need for greater and different patterns of cooperation has emerged as the world grapples with more challenging and complex problems – wicked problems.

TOWARDS AN AID STRATEGY 55

Figure 1: BRIC Countries' Aid Governance Models

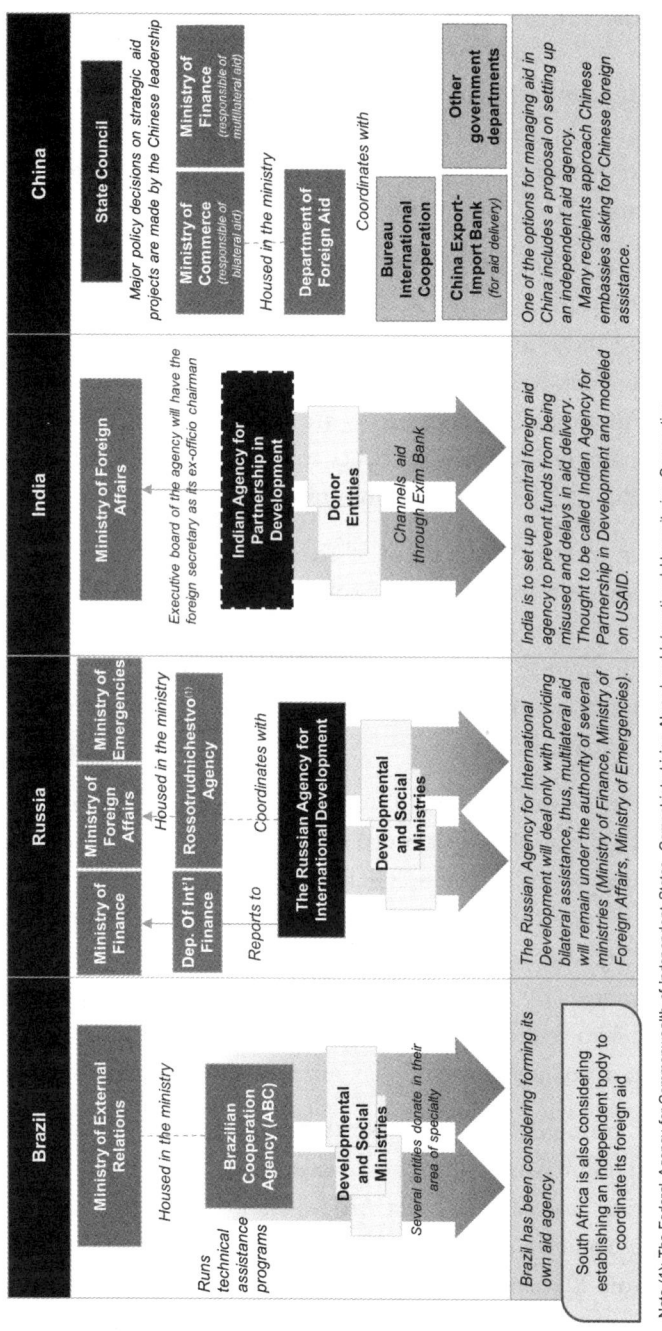

Brazil	Russia	India	China
Ministry of External Relations — Housed in the ministry	**Ministry of Finance** / **Ministry of Foreign Affairs** / **Ministry of Emergencies**[1] — Housed in the ministry	**Ministry of Foreign Affairs** — Executive board of the agency will have the foreign secretary as its ex-officio chairman	**State Council** — Major policy decisions on strategic aid projects are made by the Chinese leadership
Brazilian Cooperation Agency (ABC) — Runs technical assistance programs	**Dep. Of Int'l Finance** Reports to **Rossotrudnichestvo**[1] **Agency** Coordinates with	**Indian Agency for Partnership in Development**	**Ministry of Commerce** (responsible for bilateral aid) — Housed in the ministry; **Department of Foreign Aid** — Coordinates with **Ministry of Finance** (responsible for multilateral aid)
Developmental and Social Ministries — Several entities donate in their area of specialty	**Developmental and Social Ministries**	**Donor Entities** — Channels aid through Exim Bank	**Bureau International Cooperation**; **China Export-Import Bank** (for aid delivery); **Other government departments**
Brazil has been considering forming its own aid agency. South Africa is also considering establishing an independent body to coordinate its foreign aid	The Russian Agency for International Development will deal only with providing bilateral assistance, thus, multilateral aid will remain under the authority of several ministries (Ministry of Finance, Ministry of Foreign Affairs, Ministry of Emergencies).	India is to set up a central foreign aid agency to prevent funds from being misused and delays in aid delivery. Thought to be called Indian Agency for Partnership in Development and modeled on USAID.	One of the options for managing aid in China includes a proposal on setting up an independent aid agency. Many recipients approach Chinese embassies asking for Chinese foreign assistance.

Note (1): The Federal Agency for Commonwealth of Independent States, Compatriots Living Abroad and International Humanitarian Cooperation
Source: China White Paper on Aid, 2011; Russia's Presidential Decree "On some issues of governance in the field of international cooperation"; Literature Review

Today, the aid cooperation picture has become more complicated as it becomes increasingly common for donor countries to collaborate with other donor countries on ODA, in what has become known as triangular cooperation. In these arrangements the countries may pool resources. This cooperation might simply cover financial resources, or the technical expertise or know-how of one of the donors.

More than two-thirds of DAC countries are involved in some sort of cooperative aid initiative. We live in an era when recipient countries are becoming more involved in the implementation of aid programs, when developing countries once considered solely as recipients of aid are emerging as donors, and when all parties are focusing on the broader concept of development effectiveness. It makes sense for countries to team up, and it is also making regional distinctions more blurred.

Consider the two main types of triangular cooperation. North-North-South flows are the product of collaboration that involves the cooperation of two major donors from developed countries. ODA resulting from collaboration that involves two developing-country donors are termed North-South-South flows.[49] (Most recently South-South-South cooperation has emerged).

With North-North-South aid flows, multiple DAC countries may be involved; they may pool their contributions to increase the amount of aid donated for a particular developmental goal. Alternatively they may divide up aspects of the aid implementation according to the different resources they intend to commit to the process, or the areas of expertise that they possess. Furthermore, DAC countries that are involved in the implementation of North-North-South aid may peer-review initiatives in order to evaluate the aid work of collaborators and maximize the value of collective initiatives.

A good example of a North-North-South aid project is Denmark and Sweden's joint work to improve water management and water supplies in Burkina Faso, a poor West African nation. Together, the five Nordic countries sometimes provide aid through a multilateral institution called the Nordic Development Fund, which mirrors the donors' priorities of reducing poverty and countering the effects of climate change.

Unlike the multiple DAC members involved in North-North-South aid, with North-South-South cooperation only one DAC member needs to be involved. This type of aid, also known as triangular cooperation and becoming increasingly common, is based on the idea that the effectiveness of aid is greatly enhanced by pairing an experienced donor – this will usually mean a donor that is in the DAC – with a so-called 'pivotal' country to support the development of beneficiary countries. The role of the pivotal country in this arrangement is as a natural implementer of aid to the recipient country; usually because of the pivotal country's geographical proximity, historical ties, or shared culture or language.

Take the example of Canada, a DAC member, linking up with South Africa to deliver aid to three post-conflict countries in Africa – Burundi, Rwanda, and Southern Sudan. In this case Canada financed the training of public service managers in the African countries, while South Africa, acting as the pivotal country, implemented the training through a management academy in Pretoria.

The triangular cooperation arrangement allows for harmonization of aid implementation, and for countries to meet aid objectives in recipient countries where they may encounter barriers through a lack of understanding of local cultural norms or language. It also allows countries to get involved in projects where they do not possess the necessary technical know-how required to deliver aid objectives.

A possible drawback is if the number of donors involved begins to make the arrangement unwieldy. Collaborative endeavors of this nature must be carefully managed to make sure that the interests of the donors are aligned, that the desire for recognition and reputational benefits does not obstruct cooperation, and that the technical know-how is being used in the best way on the ground.

While much of this discussion of international governance and management of aid focuses on the behavior of donor countries, recipient countries can also play an important role in increasing aid effectiveness. The greater the alignment and cooperation with donors, for example, the more likely aid will be effective. For example, Colombia's National Development plan of 2010 specifically set out improving and diversifying international cooperation as one of its objectives. The connection was explicitly made between improvements in international cooperation and Colombia's performance on sustainable growth, regional development and social integration, and good governance. To support the government's objectives a new body, the Presidential Co-operation Agency, was created. One of its functions was to help ensure that international aid aligned with the National Development Plan – notably in three main areas of focus: jobs, poverty, and security. It was also responsible for internal coordination across business sectors and national regions in order to maximize the impact of foreign aid.

The value of cooperation is reflected in the attention it has received at aid conferences and in research papers. At the Fourth High Level Forum on Aid Effectiveness at Busan, South Korea in November 2011, for example, a collection of shared principles aimed at improving the effectiveness of development aid cooperation were agreed – the Busan Partnership agreement.

The shared principles include agreement that developing countries should define their own development models; that achieving sustainable impact is the overarching policy goal; that effective development requires the involvement of the members of the development aid ecosystem; and that transparency and accountability underpin effective development cooperation.

The Global Partnership for Effective Development Co-operation was established as a mechanism for ensuring accountability at a political level for implementation of the commitments agreed to under the Busan Partnership.[50]

Implementation

Issues relating to the implementation of aid programs are also part of the governance and management challenges that donors and recipients face. One of the most important aspects of implementation is staffing. The main decision to be made here is whether the work on the ground in the recipient country will be carried out by expatriate or local staff.

Should the donor send its own people in on the ground to administer its aid program in the recipient country or should it try to cooperate and coordinate with different NGOs to deliver the aid on the ground instead? And if so, what types of NGO? Should the agency partner with international NGOs, work with their own NGOs overseas, or work with local NGOs, ones that have local experience? (Many agencies do a mix of all three.) In reality, most donors use both expatriates and local staff; it is more a question of the balance. With respect to the field operations of the DAC countries, most of them prefer a majority of local staff, varying from the UK's position where it has had a 49/51 percent expatriate/local split, to Switzerland's implementation with a 11/89 percent split. The one outlier is France where they have had a split of 20 percent local staff and 80 percent expatriate in the past.

The difficulty with donor countries sending out expatriates as staff is that they may not be attuned to the local culture of the recipient country. The expatriates may be perceived as outsiders exploiting the recipient country and dictating what is happening, rather than aiding it in a collaborative way. As a result the expatriate staff may encounter resistance that obstructs the cooperation needed on the ground in order for the aid to be effective. In addition, the likelihood is that the more expatriates are used on the ground, the greater the costs.

There are also the elements of responsibility and accountability to consider. The greater the involvement of the donor country on the ground in terms of staffing, the greater the efforts required in terms of accountability and responsibility of those operations. With more local people involved, there is a greater feeling of inclusion, and sense that the recipient country has control of its own destiny and the development work that will help to shape that future. It may be easier to get things done, as well, as local people will understand the way things work in order to make the best progress.

One obvious trend relating to staffing is the changes in the skills required of those who are involved on the ground. So, for example, there is increasing demand for people with multidisciplinary development backgrounds. This shift in skills that are in demand reflects the increasing attention that donors are paying to development effectiveness versus aid effectiveness, the former being a broader context for ODA.

Where donor countries choose to work with and through NGOs and local networks it provides them with the opportunity for greater reach, and the ability to target the aid on the areas that the donor wants to focus on, but might not know how to access. However, there are also challenges when working with local NGOs. Deciding which NGOs to work with can be an issue, for example. There are many thousands of NGOs. Which ones do you go with? Which have the right reputation? How do you screen them? Many donors will have tried to implement aid programs with NGOs, where the NGO they selected subsequently turned out to be ineffective. So it is important for donor countries to understand the NGO landscape on the ground.

Financing

An additional and critical aspect of governance to which donors and recipients should pay attention to is the method of financing the aid, and how that financing is governed. The way that donor countries approach the issue of financing will affect the flexibility of the aid program and the ability to monitor aid effectiveness later on.

In DAC member countries there are two main ways of financing aid: budget appropriations and decentralized cooperation. With budget appropriations, the governing bodies of DAC member nations have to pass the aid program on an annual basis. These budgetary approvals are renewed every year. There is usually some flexibility to provide for emergencies, such as humanitarian crises. However, inevitably there is some tension between the need for long-term planning and the periodic approval of aid budgets.

Long-term aid plans are vulnerable to political or economic changes where they affect the DAC donor. Aid managers are also under a lot of pressure to adopt a short-term approach to aid because they can be faced with a situation where, if they do not use the entire aid budget that is available, they risk losing it. So they are under pressure to commit and disburse funds before time runs out.

A second approach to financing aid is by a decentralized cooperation mechanism. With this method, part of a donor country – it may be a region of the country or a municipality – gets involved with managing part of a country's aid agenda, often by working on shared development priorities with partner countries.

In some European countries, there is some decentralization of aid money dealt with at the provincial level. The funding may come from the national government, or it may come from an international aid organization like the United Nations or World Bank. Decentralized cooperation has gained some traction because the local expertise can sometimes be superior to that available at higher levels of government. This is often true, for instance, when the aid relates to education.

One example of decentralized cooperation is Spain. For the last three decades the country has been one of the few OECD countries to administer a significant proportion of its aid through public institutions that are not part of its central administration. In 2005, for example, this figure had reached some 16 percent of total ODA. These institutions included agencies representing autonomous communities, including Valencia and Catalonia, for example. Within these communities there are regional development cooperation funds, and development cooperation councils. Regional development cooperation funds are 'non-profit organizations, which bring together and coordinate town halls, provincial governments, and other public and private institutions, with the aim of creating an economic fund to contribute to the development of poor countries, and carry out campaigns to raise awareness about the causes of poverty and inequality.'

If the desire to give aid is an attribute of civil society then a decentralized approach, allowing local citizens to have more say, may be more appropriate than handing responsibility to central government.

The method of financing will also have an impact on transparency and accountability. With many of the more democratic donor nations, aid budgets set by government will carry with them an element of accountability to the public. Thus the degree of flexibility around financing upfront may have an impact, in terms of accountability and the need to monitoring aid effectiveness, later on.

Aid can be appropriated with different levels of control. The most stringent level of aid appropriation is where a governing body in a DAC donor country – whether that is congress or parliament, for example – specifies geographic allocations, including levels of aid for particular countries or regions, along with the use of aid (after reviewing aid agencies' proposals).

In these appropriation processes, attention is usually paid to several factors in the target country: the level of political freedom; the target country's access to credit; and the amount the target government already spends on development. The spending limits on funding activities will be set centrally by a committee that is overseen by the donor country's government. If there are any unexpected contingencies, such as a natural disaster that requires a humanitarian relief response, then these may trigger requests for additional appropriations. But these requests must be approved by the DAC donor country's governing body.

In donor countries that operate a moderately stringent approach to aid appropriation, the funding entities and senior aid officials have a degree of flexibility in adjusting allocations. Targets for moderately stringent allocation processes are usually poorer countries, with low levels of development and GNP per capita. Funding decisions are decentralized, but constrained within a framework that has already agreed priorities.

A certain percentage of funds is often reserved for emergency aid – for instance, to poor countries that have suffered some sort of natural catastrophe. Canada and the Netherlands both have moderately stringent approaches to doing budget appropriations.

Where donor countries operate a more flexible approach to aid appropriation they will approve their annual ODA budgets without immediately allocating the funds. The ultimate decisions about fund allocation will be made by the foreign affairs ministry or other bodies, either based on committee recommendations or, occasionally, in the case of emergencies, on proposals from NGOs. For example, Austria has operated a system in which at least eight ministries fund aid-related activities from their own budgets. Potentially, the country's ODA strategy might benefit from a more integrated and centralized approach. However, although fragmented between ministries, in practice at least the Ministry of Foreign Affairs, ADA (a limited company owned by the government) and the Ministry of Finance are the main bodies involved in development cooperation.

Allocation

The third pillar of any aid strategy will be how the donor country decides to allocate its available aid. This covers the delivery channels that the country will employ, and whether the donor country will deliver aid bilaterally (directly to a recipient country) or multilaterally (delivering aid in conjunction with other donors, and often through a third party organization such as the United Nations).

The delivery channel is usually the headquarters of the aid organization, but with implementation handled by a donor country, the recipient government or civil society organizations (NGOs), working to advance countries' common interests, though outside of any government or business structure.

While most DAC donor countries have not used Civil Society Organizations (CSO) to any great extent to channel aid, there has been a slight increase in their use in recent years. During the period 2008 to 2011 some $17.3 billion annually on average was channeled through CSOs by DAC members. In 2011, however, that figure rose to $19.3 billion. This was the equivalent of 14.4 percent of the DAC members' total ODA.

Where CSOs were used, they were overwhelmingly based in the donor country rather than in developing countries. And, in the case of bilateral aid, this tends to be directed at improving social infrastructure and services.

The use of CSOs does offer some benefits. CSOs are independent, and as such they are able to actively promote the interests and rights of the citizens that they represent. On the other hand, once CSOs are involved the complexity of relationships and issues around accountability can complicate matters. In addition, many CSOs are small and lack capacity and structure. It is also hard to screen which CSOs are effective and which are not. Nevertheless, some countries, such as the Netherlands (21 percent) and the US (18 percent), make more extensive use of CSOs as an aid channel.

Bilateral and multilateral donations

One of the most important decisions for a donor country when devising an aid strategy is how to deliver aid – whether to deliver aid bilaterally, as a direct transaction with a recipient country, or multilaterally, where aid money is put into a central pot and this pool of aid money is then managed by an international agency, such as UNICEF or the Asian Development Bank.

Bilateral aid is the preferred mechanism among many of the world's biggest donors for several reasons. Relationship development is one advantage, as bilateral transactions allow the donor country to obtain more exposure and credit for the aid they provide. There is also a benefit for the donor country in a bilateral arrangement with respect to control. In a direct transaction, the donor country can maintain a relatively high level of control, and has a better chance of determining how the aid is used. Moreover, bilateral aid promotes economic self-interest, especially in cases of tied aid, where the money is contingent on the recipient country spending it on goods and services that are produced in the donor country.

DAC countries dispense most of their aid in a bilateral fashion. But bilateral aid is not without its challenges. Bilateral aid sometimes travels in a herd. There are times when donor countries move en masse: when they are responding to a natural disaster, for example, or helping a newly established state. Alternatively, they may all exit a country together following a change in regime.

This collective movement of aid in or out of a country can create big swings in aid, sometimes overwhelming countries when the movement is inwards, where there is no mechanism for deploying the aid efficiently, or devastating countries when donors exit a country.

Multilateral aid also offers a number of advantages to donor countries. In general, multilateral aid is intended for developmental purposes. That includes bringing economic, environmental, and social improvements to countries that are poor or have recently been through wars. It is true that, unlike bilateral aid, multilateral aid means that the donor countries do relinquish some control over the use of the aid when they contribute aid to a multilateral organization, such as the United Nations or World Bank, for example. However, multilateral aid allows donor countries to facilitate large-scale transnational programs in a way that individual donor countries cannot. Another benefit of multilateral aid is that, because the combined funds are managed by a single agency, there are economies of scale available to the donor country as a result. Finally, multilateral aid can be highly cost-effective for the donor country, relieving it of the need to provide implementation support.

For smaller countries there are advantages in using multinationals to distribute their aid, as it affords them access to the networks and capabilities that multilateral institutions already have in place. However, while there are cost advantages available for donor countries, for smaller countries multilateral aid can prove costly because of the administrative fees charged by multilaterals.

Other characteristics of multilateral aid, compared to bilateral aid, include a greater focus on regions like Sub-Saharan Africa and South and Central Asia, and on reducing poverty. Typically, multilateral aid is less focused on education and humanitarian goals than bilateral aid.

While bilateral aid may be the favored option for many of the large donors, DAC countries do have strategies that they deploy to increase the effectiveness of their multilateral aid. These range from the careful selection of multilateral partners to the setting of key targets. These strategies may be collated and expressed in a single strategy document or found scattered across several different documents.

The DAC member countries have adopted several different approaches to maximizing the impact of their multilateral aid. One approach focuses on the selection process, with a single overall strategy that stipulates in some detail what a donor should look for in a multilateral partner.

For instance, Sweden has produced a document titled 'Strategy for Multilateral Development Cooperation'. This outlines a set of criteria that any multilateral organization must focus on when allocating aid on behalf of Sweden. At the same time the document also provides a number of tools to help Swedish aid officials determine whether or not a multilateral organization's goals are compatible with Sweden's aid objectives.

In Switzerland the approach to multilateral partner selection is outlined in the 'Switzerland's Multilateral Development Cooperation Strategy' document. This strategy document recommends that any multilateral partners should have objectives that are synergistic with Switzerland's bilateral aid objectives, and the document also defines the types of coordination that are most desirable.

Unlike Sweden or Switzerland, the United Kingdom does not tend to outline its multilateral strategy in a single document. In the past it has conducted a multilateral aid review exercise, in which several individual strategies were used to allocate ODA to multilateral organizations based on their strategies and objectives. While there is no single document to refer to, this approach does involve defining the objectives of any UK-multilateral partnership, and also provides a plan to assess the progress that has been made with delivering the UK's aid objectives.

Forms of disbursement

Another issue for donor countries, related to the allocation of aid, is the form in which aid is actually disbursed. Donors must decide whether to disburse aid through loans or grants, untied aid or tied aid. In many non-DAC countries such as China, for example, tied aid is still common.

With respect to the choice between grants or loans, grants are typically favored over loans. Grants are where the donor provides a sum of money with no obligation for the repayment of that money. The use of grants is usually motivated by the idea that the recipient should be funded but should be able to operate with reasonable independence. So the use of grants reduces the financial burden placed on the recipient country and promotes local activity in that country. At the same time there will usually be requirements and standards set by a governing body describing how recipients should spend the money.

An alternative form of disbursement is a concessional loan. Often referred to as a soft loan, concessional loans offer subsidized credit, usually to low-income countries. These loans are offered at lower interest rates and with longer repayment periods than a typical or standard market or multilateral loans. Loans may also have numerous conditions attached.

Loans and grants have different strengths and weaknesses. For instance, because they come with stringent conditions, conditional loans reduce the potential for moral hazard, as recipients are unable to obtain more money if they fail to meet the loan terms. However, those terms and restrictions also make conditional loans more complicated to administer, as the donor country will need to monitor the use of the loan money to ensure that it is being used as agreed. Most other forms of assistance come with fewer conditions, and as a result are easier to provide. However, because grants are easier to provide there may be a lack of oversight which can cause problems in terms of monitoring the aid's effectiveness later on. Most DAC donors have replaced loans with grants, opting for the form of aid that places less of a burden on recipients. For emerging economy countries that are providing aid, though, loans are still popular.

It is also worth mentioning in-kind assistance, which is the provision of resources such as food and clothing as emergency assistance, and technical assistance where aid is provided in the form of technical know-how.

Another key decision for aid strategists in donor countries is whether or not to attach certain obligations to the provision of aid. Tied aid refers to economic assistance that comes with a quid pro quo. So, for example, aid is provided on the basis that procurement contracts will be awarded to contractors or other entities in the donor country. If a donor country is providing aid to build a road, for example, then companies from the donor country will be awarded contracts to build the road.

China, a comparatively new player in the ODA ecosystem, is an extreme example of tied aid. When providing aid to African countries, for example, China gets its own companies and their employees into the African countries to which it provides aid. China might argue that there are advantages to this approach, not least in terms of lower overall labor costs, speed, and even knowledge and capability transfer.

The DAC, however, favors a different approach. In 2001, the DAC issued a recommendation that the practice of tying aid should be ended, at least in the case of poor recipient countries, the argument being that the intention of aid is to generate employment for the people in the recipient country, and to provide a process that allows for companies within the recipient country to bid for things. Untied aid ensures economic opportunity for the recipient, rather than benefits for the donor.

There is some debate over the strength of commitment to untied aid. Certainly many DAC donors have made progress on complying with the recommendation, freeing recipient countries from the obligation to buy goods and services from their aid benefactors. By 2008, tied aid accounted for just 18 percent of all DAC bilateral aid, compared with 54 percent in 2001 when the recommendation was formulated. However, a year later, 67 percent of aid from Greece and 54 percent of aid from Austria was tied.[51] And in 2011 a report from the European Network on Debt and Development estimated that at least 20 percent of bilateral aid was still tied.[52]

China is a good example of how it is possible to disburse funding in a variety of ways, some of which may qualify as ODA, while other methods used do not. Deborah Bräutigam, Professor of International Political Economy at Johns Hopkins University's School of Advanced International Studies in Washington, notes that China provides development assistance in several forms in Africa. These include 'grants, zero-interest loans, debt relief, and concessional loans,' and also 'preferential export credits, market-rate export buyers' credits, and commercial loans from Chinese banks.' In addition, China uses the China–Africa Development Fund to channel funding to Chinese companies investing in Africa, as well as lending funds to African small and medium enterprises, via African banks.[53]

Monitoring and evaluation

The fourth pillar of any aid strategy should be the establishment of monitoring and evaluation mechanisms that allow the donor countries to assess the quality of their aid programs. To understand how their aid programs are doing, donor countries usually devise monitoring mechanisms to evaluate the cost and effectiveness of administering their programs. These mechanisms vary in the degree of oversight that they provide.

The OECD Development Assistance Committee has produced a set of good-practice guidelines for the evaluation of aid programs. The guidelines, based on six general principles, have influenced the way that many donor countries approach the assessment of aid impact and effectiveness. According to the principles, for example, aid evaluation should be impartial, independent, widely disseminated, used as feedback, conducted cooperatively between donor and recipient agencies, and incorporated from the outset. Evaluations can use effectiveness, efficiency, impact, relevance, and sustainability as criteria for evaluation.

In practice, notwithstanding the guidelines, the rigor with which DAC countries monitor and evaluate the effectiveness of their aid varies widely.

Some monitoring mechanisms are highly systematic. This might include, for example, oversight by dedicated committees and agencies, and regularly scheduled reviews. Both the United States and the UK, two of the leading aid donors in the world, have adopted highly systematic approaches to the measurement of aid effectiveness, including regular reviews by bodies that are independent of any entities actually implementing the aid activity. The aim of this type of approach is to ensure objective assessment.

In the DAC, members do peer reviews – in-depth examinations of policies – in a process which can provide valuable insights that enable an improvement of aid effectiveness. Other DAC countries, such as the Netherlands and Australia, for example, have moderately organized systems. These might include objective evaluations of aid performance from external entities, for example, but the reviews would be less frequent than with highly systemic monitoring.

Finally, some donor countries adopt a relatively loose approach to monitoring aid effectiveness. They might, for example, have less concern for objectivity and allow the monitoring to be undertaken by a unit within the entity that is actually administering the aid. A few DAC countries, such as Japan and Korea, have tended to monitor aid effectiveness more loosely, with few formal requirements and without a well-developed capacity for evaluation.

Monitoring plays an important role in an aid strategy. Aid partners don't always live up to their commitments. Even when they do, the aid delivered on the ground may turn out to be fragmented and aimed at too many different objectives to make a real difference. Occasionally, aid may not even reach the people it was supposed to help. And, even when it does reach those people, overlaps and inefficiencies can make the aid far less effective. Establishing a robust monitoring and evaluation system with a reliable feedback loop allows donor countries to detect and remedy these barriers to aid effectiveness. It may lead to incremental changes within a certain process or on a particular project. It may mean altering one small but ineffective element of the aid strategy.

Alternatively, rather than incremental improvement, the monitoring and evaluation process may lead to wholesale changes, with the donor country totally rethinking its aid approach. Is it providing aid to the right countries? Is it funding the most appropriate projects? Are the project methods right? Is it partnering with the best NGOs? These questions will all form part of that evaluation process.

Regardless of the approach of the donor countries, monitoring is an essential aspect of aid strategy, if only because of the reputational risk that countries are exposed to through their aid programs. A donor country may, for example, help to finance a group of hospitals around the world in developing economies as part of a health-oriented aid program. If the hospitals are poorly managed and do not perform well, that is likely to reflect badly on the donor and potentially damage the donor country's reputation.

5
An aid roadmap

As we have seen, regardless of the progress and growth of many economies, a significant number of countries still have a pressing need for developmental aid. Fortunately, many countries, notably the members of the DAC, are both committed to providing that aid, and providing it with no or few strings attached in terms of reciprocal economic obligations on the part of the recipients.

Some countries have adopted a less altruistic and more geopolitical approach to some or all of the aid they provide. This is particularly evident with the approach of China, but also in DAC countries (although more implicitly). The emergence of China as a major provider of aid is symbolic of a changing aid landscape. As we have seen, China has a very distinct approach to its provision of aid that favors tying aid to domestic geopolitical and economic objectives.

There is change elsewhere too, as countries that were once recipients of aid become donors. India, for example, receives billions of dollars of aid annually, yet at the same time in 2013 earmarked some $1.3 billion for foreign assistance in 2013–14. This represents a 32 percent year-on-year increase in its foreign aid budget over four years.[54]

Just as they are assuming more powerful positions in the world economy, developing nations are assuming more responsibility for ODA. This challenge comes at a time when many major donors are rethinking the hallmarks of effective aid. Increasingly, instead of being evaluated on a project-by-project basis, aid is being evaluated for its overall development impact in the target community or society.

Even when the world's economic and geopolitical structure was less in flux, there was no foolproof formula for conducting an international aid program. Today, the situation is more complicated than ever. Emerging donors must figure out how to manage their aid contributions effectively. Only by understanding the challenges of ODA and how other countries are solving them, will these new donors make a major difference to their people's future and to the futures of the people who inhabit the countries to which they give aid.

Naturally, emerging players in the area of ODA want to get the most from their aid efforts. This means adopting a strategic approach to aid. There are steps that donors can take and areas in which they must make key decisions if they want to pursue a greater good of providing effective overseas development aid.

SELFISH OR SELFLESS?

Perhaps the first step for a donor country trying to develop a more effective ODA strategy, is to decide on the aid objectives it wants to pursue and the recipient countries it wants to target with its aid. Broadly speaking, a country's aid can be provided with two motives in mind: either altruistic or non-altruistic.

Altruistic aid is primarily meant to benefit the recipients of the aid, rather than the donors. This type of aid includes developmental grants and loans, including those designed to fight poverty or build infrastructure in particular areas, and includes health and education. Humanitarian goals, including reconstruction in countries after a war or natural disaster, also come under the heading of altruistic aid.

Non-altruistic aid is more about the economic or geopolitical gains that the donor country is able to obtain through the provision of aid. These might be in the area of trade and investment, be related to security, or could involve soft power, which is an increasingly common approach to gaining influence over other countries.

WHICH COUNTRIES SHOULD BENEFIT?

Once a donor country has decided on the altruistic/non-altruistic balance of its aid programs, it is in a position to decide which countries it wants to help. A straightforward method of doing this is to use a set of decision trees.

The process begins by applying a set of filters that are important to the donor country. For instance, if the donor is interested in helping countries that have developmental needs, it might screen out countries that already have good social, health, and education programs. If the donor wants to strengthen aspects of its own economy, it might screen out prospects that don't offer new markets of interest or provide it with strong investment opportunities.

Final decisions might incorporate the donor's sense of how likely it would be to achieve its aid goals and the extent to which its aid efforts might be overshadowed by the presence of another donor country already providing aid to the intended recipient. Obviously a donor country would adjust the decision factors to reflect its own priorities.

STRATEGY VIA POLICY, LEGISLATION, OR BOTH?

Strategy can be set out by being enshrined in law through the legislative and regulatory process, or it can be designated by policy statements, without being given the force of law.

Policy statements in the form of white papers, ministerial statements and multi-year master plans use guidelines and organizing principles to communicate priorities. They tend to be flexible and non-bureaucratic, thus reducing inefficiencies and delays. However, they are vulnerable to changes in political parties. This can undermine the stability of those programs.

When ODA is determined by legislation, when it is a function of a government-approved law, then the principles, guidelines and even aid amounts tend to be more rigid. This has the advantage of providing stability and a clear direction, but can be a disadvantage when external and internal events mean that a more flexible and adaptive response is required.

DONOR COORDINATION

A country that is new to ODA must decide whether, and how, to coordinate its internal aid activities. If the donor country believes that coordination will be an advantage then there are two ways that this can be accomplished.

The donor country can designate an entity to be the 'owner' of the aid strategy. This might mean establishing a new entity to play this role, or giving the job to an existing entity. Alternatively, the donor can choose not to assign an institutional owner per se, but instead look for mechanisms, such as an online infrastructure platform, to enhance cooperation and coordination.

Countries may also legitimately decide that coordination will create too big a burden, and not push for it. In this case, there is a higher likelihood of duplication and waste, and the donor's aid may be less effective as a result.

EXTERNAL COOPERATION

There are good reasons for a less experienced donor to coordinate with other donors, whether in a South-South arrangement or a North-South arrangement, where the other donors would be DAC members or the DAC as a whole.

To start with, these situations often result in greater effectiveness of aid. In addition, the donor's involvement, in its side-by-side work with other donors, may improve its international reputation.

On the other hand, teaming up with other aid-givers in triangular cooperation may reduce the donor's visibility with the aid recipient. A donor that wants a high level of visibility with the recipient, and the flexibility that comes from funding a project completely on its own, may be better off avoiding external cooperation.

Emerging donors must also decide whether to sign the major pacts forged by the DAC. Donors who sign the Paris Declaration and Busan Agreement, for example, have to operate more transparently, sharing their strategy and evaluation results with other donor countries. That is the downside of playing by someone else's rules. The upside includes the enhanced standing from becoming a signatory, especially among nations in the West.

PEOPLE MATTER

Ultimately, all ODA is delivered by people. A donor needs to make a number of decisions about how it is going to staff its aid projects. Some donors put a lot of staff into the field. Some want to have expatriates implementing the aid program in the field; other donors prefer to use locals; others put their staff mostly in the headquarters, wherever that may be.

Some donors look for staff who have highly specialized knowledge, while other donor countries prefer generalists. And then there are donor countries that don't have a standard approach to human capital at all, but make their human capital deployment decisions on a project-by-project basis.

These human capital decisions all have implications for the design of aid programs and the costs of running them. Most importantly, they have implications for the effectiveness of ODA programs.

MULTILATERAL APPROACH

If a country decides to distribute some of its aid multilaterally, then it will need to consider how it is going to approach this multilateral arrangement. It will need to decide, for example, whether to assign the strategy formulation task to a single owner, or have several entities share the job. A single owner has the advantage of being more efficient in terms of time and resources; a multiple-owner approach offers greater opportunity for customization.

The other big decision, for an aid player looking to distribute some of its aid multilaterally, is whether to create a single unified strategy for that aid, or several customized strategies to address different multilateral channels. A unified strategy has the advantage of offering a clear direction and of ensuring harmonization, though a set of customized strategies may be more effective.

And some countries may choose not to have any advance strategy at all for their multilateral aid efforts, piecing their programs together on an ad hoc basis. This has the advantage of not requiring the same level of time and resources, but can result in overlaps and inefficiencies.

FORMS OF AID

ODA can come in the form of a loan or a grant. It can be tied or untied. It can be delivered through an NGO or not.

Among the DAC, grants are typically favored over loans because the recipient assumes no financial burden, which makes it easier to pitch the program to the potential aid recipient. In addition, the conditional nature of some loans can make recipients hesitant.

Aid that is untied has also emerged as the preferred form among DAC member countries because there is no quid pro quo involved. Again, this makes the aid program an easier sell. Tied aid is more likely to be used by Southern donors. It does not have the same stigma attached if the recipient country perceives that it is getting a good deal, despite the obligations attached.

For most donors, whether or not to deliver aid through an NGO generally comes down to an analysis of the NGO's capabilities and any previous experience the donor has had with the NGO. An NGO that has a strong reputation and good reach, and which offers a low cost ratio, is often a good option.

MONITORING AND EVALUATION

Most donor countries will probably want to engage in some form of aid monitoring. A centralized model of evaluation, where a single authority creates a reporting framework and implements it across all the donor entities, is the best way of enhancing performance management at a nationwide level. However, setting up such a model requires advanced systems and considerable human resources, as well as other investments.

Hybrid models of evaluation are less demanding of the donor country's resources, as the aid entities deploy their own performance management methods but are also obliged to report chosen metrics to a common entity on a regular basis.

And then there are decentralized models of evaluation, in which each entity devises its own criteria and framework, and no attempt is made to come up with common metrics. This may be a good initial approach for new donors that want to monitor the effectiveness of their aid but do not want to spend a lot of money on monitoring.

Of course, donors have the option of not monitoring their aid programs or measuring the results of those programs. This has a cost advantage but makes it much more difficult for donors to obtain an insight into how effective the program is and make any necessary adjustments.

AVOIDING THE PITFALLS

Just as there are numerous important decisions to be made in arriving at an aid strategy, there are also several pitfalls that donor countries should avoid if they want their international aid programs to be effective, and to fulfill their aid objectives.

For example, it is important to avoid a lack of alignment with overall foreign policy. This can lead to the donor country missing the opportunity to operate its aid programs in synergy with other elements of foreign policy. It may also result in aid that is short term in nature and subject to sudden swings, either towards providing more aid or completely withdrawing it.

Another possible pitfall is the absence of long-term aid planning. This can cause programs to become fragmented and incoherent, and in doing so reduce their effectiveness while increasing their administrative costs. From a recipient's perspective, this may also result in aid that appears reactive and volatile, interfering with the recipient's ability to effectively plan how it will benefit from the aid.

Uncoordinated delivery or conflicting programs between donors must be avoided as this may lead to aid that is poorly timed, or that overwhelms local administrators, wasting resources that are needed to help a recipient when they require urgent assistance.

If there is poor program evaluation and feedback it is easy for wasteful aid programs to continue to be funded, bad practices entrenched, and therefore no improvement evident in the way aid is delivered.

A final pitfall to avoid is poor accounting of aid transactions. If aid is not accounted for properly it may give rise to ambiguity about a country's balance of payments, and lead to the overstatement of the current account balance.

Part II

Changing lives through remittances

The second of the three mighty financial forces is remittances. Simply put, a remittance is a transfer of value by a migrant from the country where they are working back to their home country – whether it is a simple cash transfer or via a more complex financial transaction.

For centuries, migrants have traveled the world hoping to create a better life for themselves and, in many cases, for the families and communities they leave behind. The total number of international migrants in 1990 was 154.1 million; in 2000 some 175 million; and by 2013 it was 247 million.[55] In 2015 over 250 million people were expected to have left their country in search of a better life.

As the numbers of migrants has grown over the years so too has the volume of money flowing to developing countries in the form of remittances. The total global value of remittance receipts for 2014 was some $583 billion.

Migrants send money home for a variety of reasons. It may just be altruistic, wanting to help the family they left behind. There may be self-interest involved, particularly if they are planning on returning home at some point. In this case they may be saving towards a target amount. There may be a balance between the migrant's target savings amount and any money required by their family.[56]

Traditionally, most remittances were sent as individual transfers and used to fund consumption of domestic purchases, such as food. In rare instances, they might be used for investment related spending (such as housing). More recently, there has been a trend towards making collective remittances in order to leverage their impact and, as well as being used to fund consumer purchases, they have been used to create sophisticated investment products, and fund development initiatives.

Such large transfers of money warrant the attention of governments in the countries from where the remittances originate as well as in the countries to which the remittances flow. Governments can do more than regulate remittances, controlling the price or means of transfer (to avoid money laundering, for example). They can also actively influence the use of remittances, whether that involves matching collective remittances, creating diaspora bonds, securitizing remittances, or promoting other innovative ways of using remittances for capital investment – funding infrastructure projects – while also improving the credit rating of the country that receives them.

This section of the book focuses on remittances and the key areas that policymakers should be aware of when developing strategies to shape the direction of remittances and their impact on development in order to maximize the beneficial effect of remittances on the lives of all citizens. For example, policymakers should be aware of which migrants are making remittances and why; the different systems that remitters can use to send money home; and the roles played by a variety of stakeholders, including local banks, international regulators, and aid agencies. Governments must also identify and evaluate their objectives and figure out what kinds of programs might help the government accomplish those goals.

As yet, many countries (both home and host) have not devised a strategy to transform these significant flows of money into the powerful government policy tool they have the potential to be. Moving in that direction means addressing several issues, not least the lack of comprehensive data on remittances, the widespread informal system of money changers that operate in many countries, and providing incentives that allow people to use their remittances for investment as well as basic consumption.

6
Migration and remittances – trends and flows

The sums involved in the global transfer of remittances are huge. As of April 2015, the World Bank estimated the total global value of remittance receipts at $583 billion for 2014, projected to rise to $636 billion in 2017.[57] A large proportion of this is the transfer of money from migrants to developing countries – $436 billion in 2014, an increase of 4.4 percent on 2013 and more than the GDP of Austria.

In India, remittances amounted to $70 billion – double the country's estimated total foreign direct investment of $35 billion.[58] In Tajikistan, in 2013, remittances represented 49 percent of GDP, with as many as half of the population of Tajik men of working-age believed to be living abroad, as is an estimated 40 percent of Somalia's population.[59] The trajectory is upwards, too.

In the short term, the World Bank expects the rate of increase in remittances to developing countries to slow down from 4.4 percent between 2013–14 to just 0.9 percent in 2014–15. This is, the World Bank notes, partly due to the poor economic outlook in some European countries that usually provide a substantial contribution to total remittances, including Russia. However, it also predicts that remittances to developing countries will pick up again, reaching $479 billion by 2017.[60]

82 THE GIVING WORLD

Figure 2: Remittances, FDI and net ODA to least developed countries (US$ billion, 1990–2014)

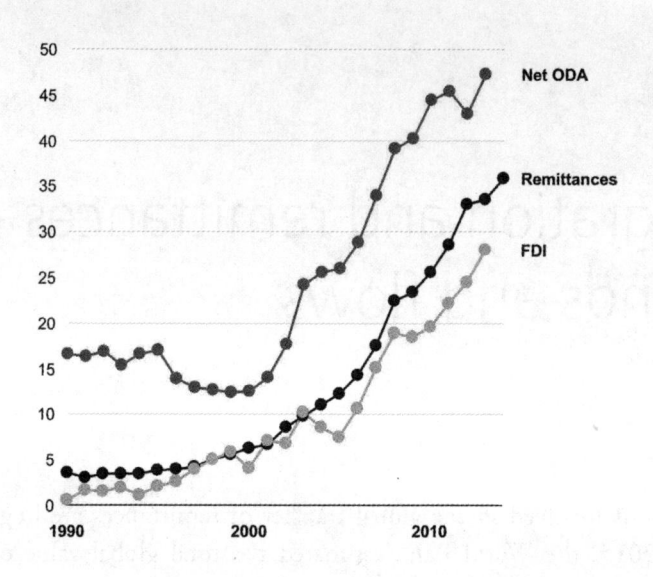

Figure 3: Remittances, FDI to developing countries and net ODA (US$ billion, 1990–2017)

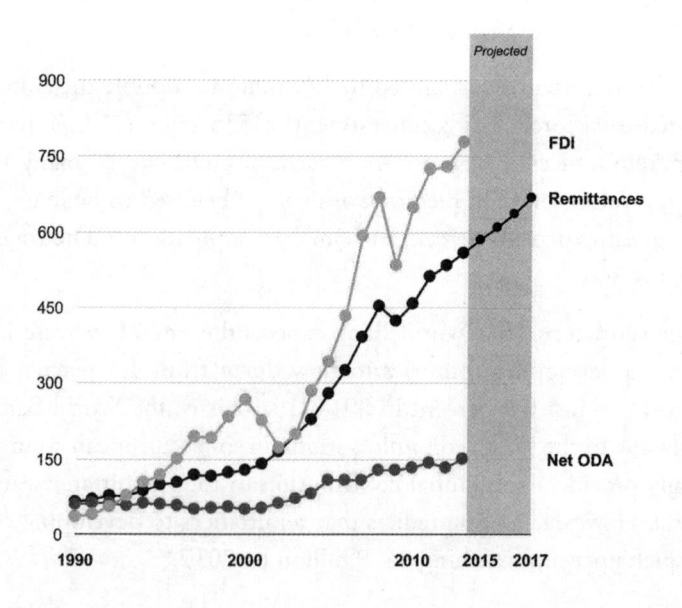

Migrants are the main source of remittance payments. Therefore, in order to fully understand the flow of remittances, and the potential for remittances to be used as a development tool by governments, it is important to look at the underlying trends regarding migration. Overall the number of international migrants has increased substantially over the last two or so decades, from 154 million in 1990 to 232 million in 2013. However, the distribution of these migrants, most notably in terms of their destination, has changed significantly.[61]

In 1990, of the total 154 million migrants, 82 million went to developed regions and 71 million to less developed regions, or 53 and 47 percent. However, by 2000 the figures were 136 million and 96 million, the proportional mix of migrants heading to developed and developing regions had changed to 59 percent and 41 percent and has remained constant since then.[62]

We can think about the relationship between patterns of migration and remittances in terms of two main types of migration: South-South migration and South-North migration.

SOUTH-SOUTH MIGRATION

South-South migration describes the movement of people from one developing nation to another.

As migrants are moving from one developing nation to another there is less of a culture shock involved than with a move from South to North. It is usually easiest for migrants from developing nations to move to neighboring countries. Indeed, roughly four in every five South-South migrants move to a country that shares a border with their home country.

There are a number of factors that drive South-South migration. One obvious motivation for people from developing countries to migrate is to improve their financial situation. This is true even in the case of migrants moving from one poor country to another.

A major push factor for South-South migration is a humanitarian crisis, such as political conflict and violence. The incidence of this type of migration varies depending on the geopolitical situation in certain regions. For example, according to population statistics from the UN's department of Economic and Social Affairs in 2013 there were some 15.6 million refugees who had left their home country, of which 13.6 million were heading for less-developed regions.

Historically, skilled labor has attempted to emigrate to the developed economies in the northern hemisphere. However, while this trend continues, more people are moving from one developing economy to another as many economies become emerging markets and home to corporations recruiting people with the kinds of skills who might previously have emigrated north.

SOUTH-NORTH MIGRATION

While South-South migration tends to be motivated by a variety of factors, South-North migration is dominantly driven by economic reasons. Most South-North migration is due to the perceived economic benefit of greater employment opportunities in the destination country, especially for highly skilled workers.

The uplift in pay and general increase in compensation and rewards available to highly skilled workers who move from developing to developed countries, usually in the OECD, is substantial. Take healthcare workers. In 2009, a comparison of healthcare wages based on purchasing power revealed that for doctors the average salary for a general practitioner in the US was $161,000 while in Mexico it was $21,000.[63] The same is true for many other jobs, from software engineers to teachers, depending on the countries involved. In fact, the socioeconomic gains for South-North migrants are considerable and extend across income, employment prospects, and health and education outcomes.

Over time migrants may return home. This is more likely to happen when incomes rise to a level they consider satisfactory in their home countries. However, as long as the substantial difference in incomes, educational standards, and other aspects of life persist between many emerging economies in the south and developing economies in the north, people are less likely to go back.

A good example is the behavior of migrants who earn PhDs in the United States. The likelihood of migrants returning home within five years is partly dependent on the economic prospects of their home country. If the PhD recipients are from South Korea, Mexico, or Brazil, for example, three countries with fast-rising income levels, then the vast majority return home within five years.

In addition, if you look at the age distribution of migrants in the North versus those in the South you find that migrants in the North tend to be older, on average nine years older, and tend to retire in the North. Of the global migrant population under the age of 20, 62 percent live in developing countries. With less disparity of lifestyle between the countries they have migrated to and from, these young migrants may be more likely to return home.

South-North migrants account for a disproportionately large share of the remittances received by all the developing countries. The country with the most migrants is the US, and the country with the greatest emigration is India. The greatest flow of remittances by total volume is from the US ($123 billion in 2012) and the biggest recipient of remittances in 2012 was India ($60 billion in 2012).[64]

Interestingly, the improved compensation levels of the South-North migrants do not mean that they necessarily send home a greater proportion of their income in remittances. If anything, evidence suggests that these migrants tend to remit much less proportionally than those at lower income levels.

REMITTANCE FLOWS

In more specific terms, regarding the flow of remittances to and from specific regions and countries within the broader South-South and South-North migration patterns, there are a number of trends.

Historically, because of their size and level of economic development, high-income OECD countries have been the source of most remittances. In 2012 remittance outflows from the US, the biggest sending country, were $123 billion. Other top ten countries with remittance flows of over $10 billion were globally dispersed covering Europe (Germany, UK, France, and Spain), the Middle East (Saudi Arabia and the UAE), Oceania (Australia), and Asia (Hong Kong).

Another tier of countries is beginning to make a greater contribution to the total flow of remittances globally. These are the so called BRIMCK countries (Brazil, Russia, India, Mexico, China, and South Korea). Between 1990 and 2008, the share of remittances from middle-income countries shot up to about 23 percent from barely 5 percent. In Brazil, for example, remittance outflows have increased from $366 million to $1 billion, while in India the amount increased from $486 million to $6.4 billion.[65]

There is another trend developing. It seems almost certain that the share of remittances being contributed by migrants in developing countries will continue to increase over the next few decades. This is particularly true where GDP growth in developing nations has outpaced growth in the more mature economies, as it has in recent years in countries including China, Vietnam, Indonesia, Brazil, and Turkey. (In the short term it will be subject to the global economic cycles, however, such as the slowing growth and mixed fortunes of emerging economies evident in 2015.)

This is accentuated by the lack of educational opportunities available in many of the high-growth developing countries. Although the situation may change as the developing countries continue to make economic progress, currently as few as one in five citizens proceeds beyond secondary education to tertiary education and postgraduate education in their home country in these high-GDP growth countries. This falls to as low as one in every ten in the Asian countries.

Demographics are likely to have a significant impact on remittance flows in the future, too. Beginning in the next 10 to 20 years, and certainly by the middle of this century, the populations in many of the mature economies will be aging, with a much higher proportion of the population over the current retirement age. The likely knock-on effect of this demographic trend is that these countries might have job openings for millions of young, highly skilled immigrants, a trend that could affect the flow of remittances.

RECIPIENT COUNTRIES

In terms of regions, East Asia and the Pacific is the region receiving the most remittance money – some $122 billion a year, according to World Bank data.[66] Within these regions, the countries that receive the most money in remittances are India, which received $70.3 billion in 2014, and China, which took in $38.8 billion in 2013.[67]

If you consider remittances as a percentage of GDP then the results vary. In Europe and Central Asia (ECA) nine countries have remittance inflows equivalent or greater than 10 percent, while in Latin America seven countries equal or exceed the 10 percent mark. At the individual country level remittances make up 49 percent of Tajikistan's GDP, 29 percent of Nepal's, 24 percent of Tonga's, 21 percent of Haiti's, and 20 percent of the Gambia's.[68]

In every recipient country, the biggest use of remittance money is the purchase of food and other essential household items. This underscores the extent to which remittances are mostly a way for migrants to share their economic good fortune with their families. In Bangladesh, for example, which is a very poor nation with one quarter of the population living on $2 or less a day, a 2011 study by the Bangladesh Bank reported that some 90 percent of remittances were used to meet basic needs, with 75 percent of households saying that they used the remittances they received for buying food.[69]

In countries with more developed economies and higher income levels, however, remittances often flow to sectors where they can have a broader impact rather than being used for food and basic amenities. This can include anything from the rebuilding of some part of the nation's infrastructure to education and investments. It is here that remittances start to intersect with some aspects of international aid, and where donor countries can try to influence the productivity of their remittance outflows.

7
Remittances – benefits and risks

As Kaushik Basu, senior vice president and chief economist of the World Bank has noted, remittances have significant potential as a policy tool, and play a crucial role in the economies of many developing countries.[70] In terms of financial flows, for example, they surpassed the contribution of international aid in the mid-1990s. Today they are second only to foreign direct investment.

As an example Basu cited Tajikistan, where remittances make up almost half the country's GDP, and Bangladesh, where they 'provide vital protection against poverty'. Or there's India, where the value of remittances in 2013 totaled almost three times its foreign direct investment in 2012.

Some have argued that, despite the considerable amount of money remitted, there is scant evidence that this translates into a positive impact on development.[71] However, given the sums involved, it seems likely that if governments can harness the economic power of remittances they can encourage its use in ways that help deliver international aid initiatives. Potentially there are considerable benefits available for both donor and recipient countries.

THE ADVANTAGES OF REMITTANCES

For a start remittances are private money flows. As private money flows, they are specifically targeted, flowing directly to the people who are intended to benefit from them. Equally, because they are private money flows to and from individuals they will not form part of a donor country's aid budget. As a result they impose a comparatively small bureaucratic burden on a donor country's taxpayers. This is an important factor. Because aid is predominantly taxpayer's money, governments are accountable for these funds. This can be an administratively cumbersome process, at times burdened by regulatory compliance and legislative oversight, for example, restricting the scope of a government's aid initiatives. Potentially, remittances offer a more flexible source of development funding.

Indeed, remittances often flow to the poorer populations in recipient countries. If this happens on a collective, pooled basis these funds can fulfill a similar function to foreign aid. They may even provide an advantage over foreign aid. These funds can be very direct in their impact. A migrant association in a donor country might collect remittances to send home to a particular village, for a particular purpose such as building a school or a hospital, for example. The use of the funds is clearly specified upfront, less money is spent on administrative costs and regulatory compliance than might be required of official aid, and more money reaches the target recipient.

This is why, when it is possible to use collective remittances, not only is it possible to use these funds as a form of aid, but also one that may prove more effective than ODA, providing there is adequate coordination between the parties, and thus effective implementation of projects. But it is also possible that scaling up remittances in this way may dilute some of the benefits that they have when made on a private, individual basis.

A third advantage for the recipient country is the nature of the flow of remittances from the donor. Aid flows are very volatile and their volume tends to depend on the economic prospects of the donor country. Take the cutting back of aid budgets following the 2008 financial crisis, for example, and commitments do not always translate into disbursements, either.

The flow of private capital into foreign countries can be unpredictable and inconsistent, too.

However, the volume and amount of remittances tend not to fluctuate as much and are likely to be more stable at times when a donor country is thinking of cutting back on aid. As *The Economist* noted, remittances have proved very resilient.[72] When the 2008 financial crisis struck, remittances to developing countries suffered a moderate downturn, declining by just 5 percent, unlike FDI and portfolio inflows in poor countries which fell by 30 percent and over 50 percent respectively. And, by 2010, remittances were regaining lost ground. This resilience is partly because of the increasingly diverse global spread of remittance providers – 46 percent were from the US back in 1970, but by 2010 that percentage was down to 17 percent.

There are also a number of broader economic benefits for the recipient country that may stem from the use of remittances. For a start, remittances are often sent to people in the recipient country with a view to them using the monies to purchase goods and services. As a result they promote growth in the recipient country by increasing consumption. In some countries, this can have a significant economic impact, although, at the same time, it has been argued that this focus on consumption limits the developmental impact of remittances. In the Philippines, for example, heavy reliance on remittances has slowed infrastructure development and jobs growth.[73]

Indeed, in some countries remittances have a very powerful effect at the macroeconomic level. They can make a significant difference to the balance of payments, and the overall financial health of a country. Remittances count as current transfers in the balance of payments and thus form part of the current account. For low-income countries that receive a considerable and relatively stable volume of remittances, those remittance payments can help to increase the overall balance of payments in the country, when taken together with exports and foreign investments. This effect is particularly important in low-income countries where, without the inward flow of remittances, there might have been a credit risk as a result of an otherwise poor balance of payments. Instead the remittance effect boosts credit ratings.

Lebanon is a good example. A 2015 report by Bank Audi noted that Lebanon's large inflow of remittances had helped it avoid the economic fate suffered by Greece. As the report noted, Lebanon's remittances to GDP ratio is some 18 percent, one of the highest in the world. Remittances make up 45 percent of total inflows, significantly greater than the 25 percent contribution from FDI. The high volume of remittance payments coming into the country has helped to keep the debt-to-GDP ratio to 132 percent, with external debt less than 13 percent of total debt. It is also worth noting that foreign currency as a proportion of total debt has fallen from 50 percent to below 40 percent.[74] Thus remittances have a very important positive impact on Lebanon's economic situation. The incoming foreign currency flows enable it to service its debts. By lowering the debt ratio, they enable the country to raise money on the international markets at a much lower rate of interest than it could otherwise do.

This effect is not only true for the Lebanon, but also the Philippines, Bangladesh and many other developing economies, where it is impossible to overlook the macroeconomic impact of remittances as the single largest source of foreign currency. For example, remittances can help prevent current account reversals, and the ensuing damage that they can cause to an economy. A current account reversal is where inflows of private foreign capital dry up suddenly. This in turn has a knock-on effect on the purchase of imports, rapidly eroding any current account deficit, and also negatively affecting the purchase of domestic goods. The result can be a devalued currency and a sharp and steep recession.

There is another less obvious benefit that the use of remittances provides for the recipient country, particularly in areas of the country where there is a low level of education and poor financial skills in the recipient population. Remittances can act as a catalyst for increasing financial literacy and financial inclusion. People who send and receive money are often prompted to become familiar with financial services that they might not use under other circumstances. As a result the transfer of money increases the level of sophistication, in terms of dealing with financial matters, of the user bases in both the donor and recipient countries.

POTENTIAL DISADVANTAGES

Of course, remittances also have their drawbacks. One potential problem with remittances for donors is that they reduce the country's level of foreign reserves. Foreign exchange reserves are used as part of a central bank's monetary policy. An outflow of remittances can impair a central bank's ability to stabilize its currency, and make it more difficult for the bank to control inflation.

In addition, many host countries feel that the outflow of remittances is money leaving the country that could have been otherwise spent in their economy. Had the remittances been retained, rather than leaving the host's economic system, they could have a larger multiplier effect internally.

At the same time, as an inward flow of money, they will have an impact on the value of the currency in the recipient country. Where they are particularly high in value, the remittances will have a similar impact to any large financial flow, causing the value of the domestic currency to rise. Thus a rising currency affects the trade deficit as it makes the recipient country's exports more expensive, and imports cheaper.

There may be also some negative social consequences that arise from the flow of remittances. For example, it may create social inequalities in some cases, between people who receive an income from remittances and those who do not.

The link between the flow of remittances and social inequality is not clear. A number of research papers touch on the issue, with arguments both for and against.[75] So, for example, in their paper 'Do remittances affect poverty and inequality? Evidence from Mali,' Flore Gubert, Thomas Lassourd, and Sandrine Mesplé-Somps note that 'whatever the simulation, we find a substantial increase in poverty and inequality under the no-migration no-remittances scenario.'

In contrast, in 'Remittances, poverty, inequality and welfare: Evidence from the Central Plateau of Burkina Faso,' Fleur Wouterse notes that while intra-African remittances reduce inequality, intercontinental remittances have the opposite effect, largely because remittances from intercontinental migration fail to reach the rural poor.

Remittances may also fuel criminal behavior. A lot of remittances are made through informal mechanisms – up to 75 percent in Africa for example.[76] This includes the informal banking arrangements of the Hawala remittance systems, used extensively throughout the world (and described in more detail on page 97). With informal remittance transactions there is no transparency or regulation. Consequently, these informal flows of money leave few trails for financial authorities to follow, and can be coopted for criminal purposes such as money laundering or financing terrorism.

Perhaps one of the most significant issues, however, is a broader challenge associated with remittances. If the volume of remittances is high it may indicate that the recipient country is failing to retain some of its most talented people at home, within its own domestic economy. If the skills and knowledge or labor of the remitter are valued and needed by the recipient country, then the money sent home may be a bittersweet reminder of the lack of opportunities for people in their home country. It may also not be adequate compensation for the costs to the economy of a shortage of skills or labor. However, the broader issue of the loss of human capital and brain drain through migration is beyond the scope of this book.

8
Sending money home

Remittances come in two basic forms. The most common form of remittance is the individual remittance. As the name suggests this is where a worker in a foreign country transfers money back to their family. Commonly, the money transferred will be used for basic purposes such as buying food or providing somewhere to live. The money may be sent back and deposited in a bank account in the worker's home country, as a kind of self-funded social security. The migrant may also use remittances as an investment in a business back in the home country.

Another, increasingly important form of remittance is collective remittances. This type of remittance is where a group of migrants from a particular country pool their money before it is repatriated. The vehicle for the transfer of collective remittances is usually some kind of organization, such as a hometown association or religious group. The organization will use the funds for a specific purpose in the home country. While the funds may be used for the development of the country more generally, the funds are often targeted for the development of a specific region, city, or town associated with the group remitting the money.

Individual remittances dwarf collective remittances in terms of volume and value. However, collective remittances have a disproportionate significance because they tend to involve development-type projects. Indeed, policymakers are increasingly considering remittances as a potential source of funding to be directed at developmental aims.

For example, take a look at how the use of remittances transferred from Mexican expatriates back to their home towns has evolved over the years. What started out with individuals making up most, if not all, of the remittances has progressed to collective remittances from households and then the increasing involvement of hometown associations (HTAs).[77] These associations, or clubs as they are commonly known, are based on social networks established by members of the same rural communities in Mexico. The role of community leaders, as well as Mexican state governments and consulates in the United States, has been instrumental in their establishment.

HTAs use remittances to promote the wellbeing of their community, both in the United States and Mexico, raising money to finance public works and social projects. There is a particular focus on the needs of people on low income living in Mexico. Investment covers a wide range of activities, but most spending is on infrastructure. When HTAs and their federations fund roads and bridges they boost local economic activity. At the same time, by financing education and health infrastructure they invest in human capital in the region.

Research shows that HTA members tend to use the most traditional informal remittance mechanisms, notably sending cash via relatives or friends. The next most common method is using money orders and other documents by mail. This highlights the issue facing many migrants – that the cost of making remittances through banks and money-wiring companies can deter them from using these methods.

And it is not only policymakers in the receiving countries, the countries to which remittances flow, who have the opportunity to capitalize on the development potential of collective remittances. As we will see, it is also possible for policymakers in donor countries to use initiatives involving collective remittances as a tool to meet their foreign aid objectives.

It important to note, though, that while this form of remittances is very promising its effectiveness is highly dependent on coordination between the local government, HTAs, and the community at large. As such, the design and implementation of projects faces similar issues to those of aid in terms of effectiveness – albeit with a higher level of targeting and possibly a greater will to make the projects work.

WAYS HOME

Migrants send money home in a number of ways. A Filipino working in America, for example, would usually send money home by using a bank, or by visiting the post office, or by using the services of a money transfer operator such as Western Union. Migrants from Moldova in Europe might choose to deliver money in person, waiting until they were back in their home country, having a meal with their family, to remit the money.

Someone from Pakistan might use the services of a Hawaladar, an unofficial money changer. The Hawaladar will arrange for the money to be delivered door-to-door to a destination in the home country of the migrant, without the involvement of any government bureaucracy. The migrant will trust them to do this reliably.

There is, therefore, a range of possible mechanisms for transferring remittances. There are formal systems that are part of both the sending and receiving country's financial services industry. There are also informal systems – for example, where someone calls at the migrant's work premises or home to pick up money, and someone else knocks on the door of the migrant's family on the other side of the world to complete the delivery. Each mode of transfer has its advantages and disadvantages.

FORMAL ROUTES

There are a number of different formal mechanisms available for transferring remittances. Banks are one obvious route for migrants sending money home. On the positive side banks are generally a reliable conduit for remittances, and are often the cheapest option for transferring large amounts of money. Many of the host countries will have extensive banking networks, and this can make it easier to find somewhere to carry out the transfer.

On the downside it can be expensive, on a percentage basis, to transfer small amounts of money through the banking system, and a lot of remittances are small payments. In Europe, for example, the typical amount of money sent by migrant workers ranges between $1,500 and $3,200 annually.[78] Those who send remittances regularly tend to send $200 to $300. Remittances per capita from European sending countries averaged $178 per capita in 2014.

And, while migrants may have easy access to banking networks when they are remitting payments, this is not necessarily true for the recipients of those payments. Not only must the sender have a bank account, but the recipient will need one too, and this can be an obstacle in some poorer countries.

Indeed, it is possible that banking policies in the sending country may inhibit the use of formal remittance systems. For instance, in order to get a bank account in Singapore, and therefore to be able to use a bank to send money home, migrants must be able to satisfy a number of criteria such as showing proof of residency or employment, showing proof of address, producing identification papers, handing over a reference from a bank in their home country, and being able to make a minimum initial deposit. Banks in other countries – such as Japan, Hong Kong, and Malaysia – also have strict prerequisites for migrants wanting to use the banking system to transfer payments home.

There is also the question of what happens if funds are lost. By using banks there should be a record of the transaction. However, as many people will have experienced in their normal dealings with banks, rectifying problems – such as lost remittances in this case – can be a cumbersome and time-consuming process.

Post office transfers are another formal option. The advantages are that post offices tend to be ubiquitous, and the remittance service is often cheaper than other formal services. However, the transfer process service via the postal office system is often slow. Furthermore, remittances sent via the post office may be further delayed at the recipient's end. This might be due to a bad postal service network or a lack of liquidity in the receiving country.

A third option for migrants who want to use a formal mechanism to remit their money is to use a money transfer operator, such as Western Union, Eurogiro, or Moneygram. These types of money transfer services are fast, usually very reliable, and easy to find in the more densely populated areas of host countries. The problem with using a money transfer operator is that the foreign exchange rates which they offer may be unfavorable compared with general market rates. And, as with the banks, money transfer operators can be expensive when sending small transactions.

More recently, smart-card companies, such as Smart-transfer, and telephone companies have also begun remittance transfers, with or without links to banks.[79] These new agencies have helped to speed up remittance transfers and provide alternative delivery mechanisms, but remittance transfer prices remain at high levels.

Credit unions are another possible remittance-transfer mechanism for migrants. These not-for-profit financial cooperatives are member owned and usually provide a range of services including savings, credit, and money transfer. Credit unions tend to be formed and used by groups of people with a common connection, whether that is community, nationality, religion, or something else. (More information about credit unions is available via the World Council of Credit Unions website at www.woccu.org.)

For those migrants who choose not to use formal channels, their decision is likely to be influenced by the perception that the formal channels are expensive, an impression almost certainly exacerbated by the bewildering number of options and fees. If someone wanted to send $200 home from South Africa to Malawi it could cost up to $65, allowing for currency exchanges and fees, depending on the service provider, and still take three to five days.[80] A Brazilian working in New York could spend as little as $12 to send $200 back to their parents – or as much as $30. Whereas someone from India could spend as little as 56 cents to send $200 home, depending on which formal mechanism was used.

In general, the cost of sending a remittance tends to be higher in host countries that do not have big remittance outflows, and higher in the South-South than the North-South corridor.

INFORMAL DELIVERY

Because of the nature of informal remittance mechanisms, statistical data on these types of transfers are scarce. Nevertheless it is clear that a significant proportion of remittances are made by informal means. Take migrants working illegally, for example. Most will resort to informal means to send money home if they choose to make remittances. There are a considerable number of illegal migrants in some of the major developed economies. In the US, for example, there are some 11.5 million illegal immigrants, while in the EU that figure was estimated at 107,365 in 2013.[81]

Perhaps the most direct informal mechanism is where the migrant takes money home in person, or sends it home with a friend or relative. However, most remittances made through informal mechanisms probably occur through the Hawala system and Hawaladars. The Hawaladars are the money changers who act as intermediaries in both the sending and receiving countries. They are often people from the same country who speak the same language as the migrants, and whom the remitters believe they can trust.

Hawala services tend to be reliable and are often a very convenient means of sending money. For example, they allow both the migrants who send the money and the recipients of the remittances to complete their transfers without having to open bank accounts, or fill out paperwork, or even leave their homes. These services are used extensively by people in developing nations, and have played a role in the rapid rise in assets experienced by Islamic banks in recent years.

Nevertheless, although informal mechanisms have their advantages, there are drawbacks for remitters too. Hawala networks are not without risks, both to the migrants remitting the money and to the countries in which they operate.

If there are disagreements between the migrant and the Hawaladar or the money is lost, somewhere en route to the family – left on a train or a bus, or stolen – the lack of any paper records puts the migrant at a big disadvantage. The migrant is likely to lose the money. And delivery in person can be a slow and inconvenient way to reach relatives, especially when they live in rural areas.

For the countries where the Hawala system operates there is also the risk of the remittances sent through the Hawala system being used for illegal activities, such as money laundering, the funding of narcotics trafficking, and financing terrorism. There are precedents for the Hawala system being used in this way. In 1993, for example, a series of bomb blasts in India were financed by Hawala operators based both abroad and in India. In 1997, a Hawala network spanning several countries was implicated in a money-laundering case involving the sale of Pakistani heroin and opium. And the terrorist attacks of September 11, 2001 intensified concerns about the activities that could be supported through the Hawala system.

Much of the focus on informal mechanisms of transfer tends to cover the negative aspects of informal remittance systems, such as the ability to channel informal remittances payments to criminal activities. However, it would be wrong to ignore the many advantages that these informal mechanisms offer, advantages that mean that they are likely to remain popular.

These informal mechanisms are often referred to as 'the poor's banking system'. For migrants, they enable the transfer of small amounts relatively cheaply, something that is often not possible through conventional banking channels. A tough regulatory environment and other barriers to entry mean that the formal transfer market is not as competitive as it could be, and prices are higher as a result.

Equally, there are other, less obvious, costs which may be less onerous in the informal market. Exchange rates are a good example, as unofficial channels are likely to offer better exchange rates than formal channels.

In addition, migrants may not trust the formal mechanisms for transferring money, even if they are available to them. And sometimes it is easier and cheaper to take the money home in person or entrust it to a friend or relative, especially where the recipients live in areas where financial services facilities are scarce.

When the costs are added up, along with the inconvenience of having to go to a bank, it should be no surprise that so many remitters take advantage of informal mechanisms to get their money home. Of a range of migrant nationalities, 80 percent of Ugandans, 54 percent of Bangladeshis, 47 percent of Moldovans and 38 percent of Armenians opt for informal remittance systems.[82]

THE VALUE OF GOVERNMENT INTERVENTION

The reconstruction work in Haiti following the earthquake in 2010 is an example of how remittances can be used for development purposes – in this case to bolster humanitarian aid efforts.

Prior to the devastating earthquake, Haiti was already the recipient of a considerable flow of money from remittances. In 2008, for example, officially recorded remittance flows were some $1.4 billion, but allowing for money sent via informal channels that figure was more likely to be in the region of $2 billion. And again in 2009, despite the global financial problems, the Haitian diaspora still contributed $1.64 billion to Haiti, or 26 percent of Haiti's GDP. That included some 300 Haitian hometown associations in the United States and Canada each donating approximately $10,000 for social projects in their home communities.

After the earthquake the US government temporarily extended protected status to Haitians already in the United States, for a period of 18 months. This meant that over 200,000 Haitians without the appropriate documents were able to work legally in the US. In turn, this meant that it was easier for these people to send remittances through formal channels back home to Haiti. The result was an increase of some $360 million in 2010, making a significant contribution to the earthquake response.[83] [84]

Remittances affect developmental outcomes when they are used to increase the wellbeing of the remitter and the recipient and, over time, of communities and regions. These are outcomes that overlap with the development agenda of governments. As a result it makes sense for governments to intervene where they can and enable remitters to achieve optimal use of their remittances in the knowledge that in doing so they are likely to be meeting their own development goals. Governments also have the resources and the bright minds needed to develop and adopt innovative interventions, leading to better development-related outcomes using remittances.

With high public debt a problem globally, and a shortage of development funding, a stable and sizeable flow of financing such as remittances presents an important opportunity for governments to make a big difference. It is worth remembering that remittance flows are in some cases (least-developing countries) greater than foreign direct investment. Intervention policies are instrumental in both changing the direction of flows and scaling up remittances, as they are often too small for individual remitters to bring about substantial change on their own, especially for the bulk of remittances originating from unskilled (and therefore less well off) labor.

So, for example, despite the private nature of remittances, there are many reasons why governments might wish to develop policies that affect the way money is remitted by migrants, not least in the hope of influencing development outcomes in a positive way.

One area that they are likely to focus on is encouraging the use of formal channels for making remittances. As outlined in the previous section choosing to use informal remittance mechanisms presents some problems for those making and receiving that remittance. However, there are also implications for governments that impact broader economic policy and the ability to optimize development policymaking decisions. For example, informal payments are not recorded in official statistics and data, leaving the unsatisfactory situation of having to formulate policy using incomplete and unreliable data.

There is also an effect on the level of broad money in the economy which will have implications on monetary policy, and because these remittances are 'hidden' it is hard to see the consequences of these informal flows of money on exchange-rate operations.

So what can governments do to make remittances more effective?

9
More effective remittances – the role of government policy

Governments can use their policies to direct remittances towards productive uses in many ways. These outcomes vary from simple increases in consumption to involvement in large-scale infrastructure projects. They include, for example, increasing the wealth and purchasing power of individuals in recipient countries, enabling people to consume more; encouraging remitters to become social entrepreneurs; encouraging the collective use of remittances for investing in larger projects at a community level; promoting the investment by remitters in government bonds which allows for this money to be pooled and used for projects at a macro scale by governments.

Primarily, government initiatives will be of two types. Passive policies are designed to facilitate the payment of remittances. The aim is to maintain a flow of remittances from the host country; however, they are not usually designed to affect the behavior of the remitter in terms of what they use their remittances for. Active policies go a step further as they are usually an attempt to direct those remittance flows to a particular target, and to make sure that the remittances have the maximum developmental impact.

With both passive and active policies, one important shared aim is to encourage migrants to remit money through more formal mechanisms. As we have seen, by their very nature, informal remittance flows are hard to track or influence in terms of their use, and it is difficult to monitor their impact. It is in the interests of governments, and in many cases both the migrants and the recipients of remittances, that migrants feel able to use formal mechanisms to send money. However, a range of measures will be required if formal mechanisms are to be more palatable.

PASSIVE POLICIES

The most basic and common remittances are transfers of money from migrants to their family members. With these remittances targeted for private and personal use, there are limits to what governments can do in terms of interventionist policies. As a result, any government policies that are directed at these types of remittance tend to be passive ones. That is to say, they tend to be policies that facilitate the flow of money between borders, and are less directed at trying to influence the goals of the remitter or the recipients of that remitter. Even with smaller remittances, however, there may still be policies that attempt to change the behavior of remitters to either give collectively or to channel their money towards more investment-oriented purposes.

Information disclosure and awareness

One of the simplest things that governments can do to facilitate the transfer of monies home is to help migrants and their families understand the formal remittance process: what services are available to them, how those services work, and what are the costs involved, for example.

A large part of this will be about explaining the channels available for migrants to send money home, and how those formal mechanisms work. This does not just mean banks, money transfer companies, or credit unions. It might include how to take advantage of new technology to make remittances, such as the use of mobile phones and payments.

The challenge is that, without this kind of information being available, there is a good chance that migrants will use informal channels to remit their money. So, by raising awareness about alternative methods of sending the money home, governments help to encourage the use of formal channels, and in doing so avoid money laundering and the illegal movement of money. While providing more information and advice about formal mechanisms for remitting money may seem straightforward, in practice it can be a challenge, not least because it may be difficult to reach those migrants who are using informal methods – many of them will be working in the shadow economy, for example.

In Mexico and the Philippines, for instance, the governments, through their overseas workers' resource centers, maintain a price database providing remittance-price information to consumers. Other countries could adopt a similar policy using the World Bank's World Remittances Prices Database which covers prices in the main migration corridors, and country-to-country information.[85]

Legislation and regulation

Another area where governments can intervene to ease the remittance of money by migrant workers is by prompting changes that allow or make it easier for savings banks, credit unions, and microfinance institutions – and other financial institutions – to play a role in remittance services.

For example, many migrants send small amounts of money back home. Because of the size of these payments it is impossible or uneconomical to send them via banks. It may even be difficult for the migrant to open a bank account in the first place. Thus, from the outset, many migrants are limited to credit unions or money transfers in their choice of formal channels.

Governments should consider how they might, through legislation and regulatory intervention, make things easier for the migrant. In a way it is similar to the situation with loans in some economies. Where banks are reluctant or unable to provide small loans, some governments have stepped in, through regulatory interventions, to facilitate government-backed micro loans to individuals who have very little money or security. So governments can adopt innovative solutions, whether through regulation or policy, to encourage banks to facilitate these payments.

In Bangladesh, India, Pakistan, and Sri Lanka, the governments have created a legislative framework that aims to encourage citizens who have emigrated to remit money back to their home country. Measures typically include allowing non-resident citizens to have bank accounts in both local currencies and foreign currencies without penalizing them through the tax system or in other ways. They may also be able to invest in local firms through securities, and own physical assets such as domestic and commercial property.

Turkey is another good example of a government that tries to facilitate the use of formal remittance systems by its non-resident citizens. Since the 1970s, when the oil crisis led to Turkey having trouble financing its current account deficit and the government took action to liberalize the economy, Turkish expats have been able to hold foreign currency accounts (the Turkish lira did not achieve full currency convertibility until 1989). Agreements were signed with various financial institutions in Europe and the US, as well as the German postal service, to allow more efficient remittances by Turkish expatriates. Furthermore, after a domestic financial crisis in 1994 which precipitated a flight of capital from the country, Turkey introduced two special Super Foreign Exchange Accounts offering longer term and better interest rates for Turkish expats. These now account for some 50 percent of Turkey's international reserves.[86]

Governments can also pass anti-money-laundering provisions; these help route remittances through official channels. Legislation has been passed in the US and the UK, for example, to prevent money laundering, but also in countries such as India, Bangladesh, and Afghanistan. The Financial Action Task Force on Money Laundering (FATF), is an intergovernmental organization set up to combat money laundering.

Competition legislation can also make a difference to remittance pricing, as more entities are encouraged into the market to provide remittances.

Facilitating the remittance process and reducing cost

It is possible for central banks to take even greater measures to facilitate the remittance process. For example, they can encourage partnerships between banks and other service providers, such as microfinance institutions and

MORE EFFECTIVE REMITTANCES – THE ROLE OF GOVERNMENT POLICY

post offices, to improve the quality of remittance service and drive down costs. Central banks can also impose ceilings on transfer fees. Facilitating the entry of more service providers into the market increases competition and can also drive down the cost.

In Turkey the banks have developed an easy to use, fast, and relatively cheap transfer system known as the passing trade system. This is a bit like a post office money transfer, as neither the remitter nor the recipient needs to have a bank account at the bank being used. In the country the remittance is being sent from, the expatriate produces identity papers that are valid in both the country of residence and in the country to which the money is being sent. The money is sent on the same day and at a lower cost compared to other formal options.

Another facility has also been introduced to compensate for the fact there is unlikely to be an extensive network of Turkish banks in the country where the remittance is being sent from. As long as the expatriate is able to deposit the money at the branch of a Turkish bank, even if it is not the same bank as that used by the recipient of the money in Turkey, the bank will still transfer the money to the recipient's 'collective' account. This is a reciprocal arrangement between Turkish banks.[87]

The collection of comprehensive data on remittance flows

In order to set effective policies it is important to have good information on which to base policy decisions. One of the challenges with remittances, certainly when it comes to governments devising remittances policies and attempting to maximize the benefits that they provide in the migrant's home country, is the lack of visibility on remittances. Many countries simply do not have quality data on remittance flows, on the value and volume of remittances, the size of payments, or their channels – in terms of the mechanisms for transferring the money, the route it takes, where it goes to, and what it is used for.

This type of information would indicate to governments the different types of migrants and how the nature of remittances varied between them, where the money was going to in terms of destination countries, and who the actual recipients were. Are remittances going to the poorer developing countries to be used for subsistence purposes? Are the remittances coming from the more highly skilled migrants, in which case large sums of money may be leaving the country where the migrants work?

When governments do have data it is often incomplete. By putting in place mechanisms that allow for the consistent collection of data over time governments will be in a better position to set effective policies relating to remittances. This applies to both donor and recipient countries.

Fostering dialogue between sending and receiving countries

Governments do not have to devise policies in isolation. Instead they may meet with other governments to share best practices and discuss how to optimize the impact of money being transferred back home by migrants, or to talk about means of making it simpler to send back money. This may not require direct cooperation between central governments.

In the US, for example, the Federal Reserve Banks offer expatriates a way to send money across borders to over 35 countries via the FedGlobal ACH payment system. Users of the system can distribute payments between deposit accounts. Alternatively they can let a recipient retrieve funds from a participating bank location or a trusted third-party provider in certain receiving countries that currently holds an account with a US depository financial institution.

In setting up the system, the Federal Reserve Banks worked with a variety of central banks and other financial institutions overseas including the Mexican central bank (Banco de México) to ensure regulatory compliance, ensure fees are kept to a minimum, and sort out other issues.[88] Dialogue can also be initiated by aid agencies, for example, and some countries are already doing this.

ACTIVE POLICIES

Alongside passive policies, governments may also set more active policies. Instead of just attempting to facilitate the flow of remittances, active policies are more interventionist. They seek to influence various aspects of the remittance process, including how these transfers of money are made, their use, and the impact that they have. Active policies are targeted to the extent that some are better suited to highly skilled migrants, while others are more suited to migrants with fewer skills.

The idea of active policies directed at remittances is partly about rebuilding economies through aggressive expenditure in areas that are much needed in a migrant's home country. One target of these policies is the high-end remitters, migrants who usually provide a lot of money but may not send remittances that often. The challenge for governments is to incentivize these better-off migrants to use their funds in a much more targeted way in order to rebuild infrastructure or make other types of large investment in their home countries.

Active policies are not solely aimed at high-end remitters, however, as it is still possible to target remitters of smaller amounts productively. Indeed, the expatriates who remit smaller sums but do so more frequently can make a huge difference if they pool their resources, using the money for entrepreneurial ventures, for example.

Encouraging investment in the receiving country's capital markets

When remittances are used to buy the debt issued by the migrant's home country it helps to improve the country's creditworthiness and benefits the economy. Another way of actively promoting the constructive use of remittances is through the issuance of diaspora bonds. Developed economies often raise money for specific projects, particularly infrastructure projects, by selling bonds to investors. However, accessing capital markets may be more difficult for developing economies, especially at reasonable interest rates. One possible alternative is to raise funds for projects via their overseas migrants.

Many higher-income migrants remain proud of their country of origin, and want to give back to their home country. One way that they can make this contribution is through so-called 'diaspora bonds'. The bonds will be issued by the recipient country in the normal way but are targeted towards, and often actively marketed to, members of the diaspora. Indeed, to be effective the issuing government must try to ensure that there is sufficient demand for such a bond, that there are enough suitable people with the means to invest in the bonds, that they can be communicated with, and that the government has the technical skills required to issue, market, and manage the bond.[89]

Migrants' desire to help often means that they are willing to buy these bonds at a premium, reducing the government's borrowing costs. In addition, diaspora bonds are usually structured as long-term debt instruments with all the interest accruing and being paid, along with the original principle, when the bonds fall due (an approach known as bullet repayment). This makes them a good source of long-term foreign financing for the countries that use them.

These types of policies are becoming more widespread. They are dependent on countries having diasporas that are very well off, patriotic in nature, and happy to give in a way that funds specific projects.

The biggest issuer of diaspora bonds is Israel, which uses the proceeds from the bond sales to finance major public sector projects such as housing, infrastructure construction, and desalination. The country sees these bonds as a stable source of overseas borrowing and as a way of maintaining ties with Jews living in other countries. The patriotic discount was particularly large in the 1970s and mid-1980s, but has been declining since. Although the bonds are aimed at native-born Israelis, people born elsewhere can still buy Israel's diaspora bonds.

India is another country that has issued diaspora bonds. Unlike Israel's bonds, only investors of Indian origin have been able to purchase the diaspora bonds issued by India. The Indian government launched these diaspora-targeted investments – in the form of Resurgent Indian Bonds and India Millennium Deposits – to support the balance of payments at times when the international capital markets have been unreceptive.

Other countries are also investigating diaspora bonds as a means to address financial shortfalls. These include Ghana, which launched a $50 million Golden Jubilee savings bond in 2007, while Ethiopia issued a second diaspora bond, the Renaissance Dam Bond, in 2011. The bond was intended to help finance the government's Grand Renaissance Dam infrastructure project.[90]

Another way that remittances can be used in connection with capital markets is through securitization. This is how it works. A bank, usually in a developing country, establishes an offshore entity called a Special Purpose Vehicle (SPV). The bank sells an asset to the SPV, in this case its right to future remittance flows. It can do this as the right to receive payments from an expatriate making a remittance payment — money wired to the bank, for example — is separate from the obligation to pay the person the remittance was intended for.

The sale of the asset creates a debt. The SVP packages up the debt and sells it to investors in the form of bonds. The proceeds are passed on to the bank. A trustee account is established into which remittances are paid. The funds that accumulate there are used to pay principal and interest to the investors; excess funds are passed to the bank.

Given the large and steady flows of remittances, there is considerable potential for securitizing remittances. The benefits are considerable. It enables access to international capital markets for poorer countries that might find that access difficult to obtain. Siting the SPV offshore means that investment-grade ratings can be obtained, often a better credit rating than the sovereign rating of the country where the originating bank is based.

Funds can be raised specifically for development, as was the case in Africa where the African Import Export bank facilitated several future flow securitizations, including one deal where it arranged for Ghana to borrow $40 million in favor of a development bank. The loan was backed by the collateralization of Western Union remittance receivables.[91]

Another benefit is that it creates an incentive for the bank to maintain and increase the future flows of remittances, and so encourages greater use of the formal remittance system.[92]

Supporting migrant associations and promoting remittance pooling

Another way that governments can promote the use of remittances as a source of investment by migrants in their home country is by encouraging the development of migrant associations.

This is where migrants band together and decide to pool their resources and send this money back through a migrant association for the community financing of infrastructure and other projects in the home country. These associations tend to be formed by migrants gathering together as a grass roots movement. There is a sense of belonging and a desire to give back that is shared between the migrants in associations. Many home associations are religious in nature, for example.

Noting the effectiveness of this method, governments in the recipient countries have offered to top up the remittance money. Rather than the money just flowing passively, the government adds a certain amount for every dollar provided by the migrants. By topping it up, the pooled fund becomes larger and potentially more useful. Also when the governments of receiving (or sending) countries are providing matching funds, it gives people who are working in the sending country a further incentive to contribute to these remittance-backed projects.

This approach to making use of migrant associations does not have to be initiated by the recipient country. It can also be used by donor countries through their aid agencies. In many cases these countries are already donating a lot of money to the recipient countries. One of the problems with aid is that it tends to be untargeted. This means there might be uncertainty about when or where the aid is going to flow and a related risk of corruption. With the home associations it is likely that many of the projects are very well targeted – so, for example, they would know that a school or a hospital was being built in a certain location.

If money from remittances via migrant associations is being earmarked for a particular project, a donor country could start topping up these remittance flows, knowing that the money is flowing for developmental reasons, rather than waiting for the recipient country to step in. This might provide an incentive for the recipient country to take action.

A good example of state intervention in a recipient country is the case of Zacatecas in Northern Mexico. During the 1970s many people from Zacatecas migrated to live and work in California and, in particular, the area around Los Angeles. Many of the Zacatecans in this area were eager to contribute to the welfare of the family members, neighbors, and friends they had left behind. They were also keen to remember their Mexican heritage and not to be seen as *pochos*, a derogatory term used to describe emigrants from Mexico who reject their cultural heritage or language.

Initially, for every peso contributed by the migrant Mexicans to the state's hometown association the state of Zacatecas also contributed a peso. The program was so successful in eliciting remittances that, during the 1990s, the federal and municipal governments decided to contribute as well. Thus the Zacatecan hometown association program became a 'Tres por Uno' program – with three additional pesos added for every peso remitted. In 2001, by which time the program had already raised $4.5 million for some 200 community projects, then-president Vicente Fox institutionalized the idea, prompting hometown associations to take root elsewhere in Mexico.

Today, the program is a four-for-one program, due to an additional commitment made by the money transfer operator Western Union. Over time these associations have, with the help of remittances from Mexicans living in the US, made possible a wide variety of projects in Mexico including the building of waste-water treatment plants, the repaving of roads, and other initiatives in environmental health, education, urban improvement, and agriculture.

Retail payment system

New technologies introduced by banks and other financial institutions can simplify the task of making remittances and provide incentives for migrants to remit money on a more formal basis. A good example is the use of cellphone-based remittance systems. Active policymaking by governments to facilitate the development and use of technology in this area is in its infancy, but growing.

In Georgia, for example, the International Organization for Migration Mission to Georgia is involved in a two-year project funded by the International Fund for Agricultural Development (IFAD), which aims to make it easier for Georgian expatriates in Greece to send money home. The project looked at cost comparisons of different money transfer technologies, including mobile phone payments. It also investigated how to link remittance payments with savings and investments schemes, as well as exploring how remittances could be tied to local government support in order to meet the needs of target communities, including funding entrepreneurial ventures.[93]

Supporting financial innovation

Another, more financially sophisticated, way for governments to actively intervene and maximize the efficiency of remittances is to create new financial instruments and products that involve remittances.

As they work with migrants to help facilitate their remittances, banks will naturally end up converting some of those people into new customers. They can then encourage those customers to become savers and investors. At the same time they may introduce remittance-linked consumer or housing loans or insurance products, for example, that can subsequently be pooled, securitized, and sold to investors.

Technical assistance

As noted previously, governments can provide information about money transfer processes in a passive way, to make it easier for migrants to remit money. However, they can also go a step further and get aid agencies to work directly with remitters to help them understand how to use remittance services. As an extension of this more active approach, they can also provide technical expertise on how migrants can save and invest in both their host and origin countries.

'Migra-loans'

In some developing economies there is evidence of a strong link between microfinance, a form of innovative financing targeted at poorer communities and migration, and remittances.

It was thought that providing access to microcredit programs and low-cost credit would, through its support of local enterprise and employment, reduce the need for and reliance on migration. However, research by Maryann Bylander, at the Department of Development Studies of the School of Oriental and African Studies at the University of London, looking at the impact of microfinance in rural Cambodia, suggests that access to these types of loans may actually enable and drive migration.

In the Chanleas Dai commune in Cambodia, migration to Thailand has long been the main means of providing an income and surviving. Yet, even as access to microcredit increased steadily from the late 1990s onwards, migration remained an integral part of the communities' livelihood strategy.

As Bylander observes, borrowing and migration often go hand in hand.[94] What she terms 'migra-loans' work in three ways in Chanleas Dai. They are used to finance the costs of migration, even though this may contravene lending policies; fund non-productive purchases, such as houses, with the intention of servicing the loan through remittances; and bail out householders with microfinance debts they cannot pay, who then have to migrate and use remittances to repay the bail-out loans.

It is also worth noting that in the case of some host countries, such as the UAE, the government offers support for laborers to help them pay debt that they might have acquired in the process of migration. This accordingly encourages remittances as it relieves migrant workers from their debts.

The evidence suggests that the risks of getting involved in local enterprises make migration more likely and local investment less likely. Despite, or indeed because of, the availability of finance, the strong culture of migrations and remittances persists. This is a pattern that has been noted elsewhere in the world, in economies such as India and Senegal.

THE INVOLVEMENT OF DONORS

As already mentioned, it is not just recipient countries that are able to use active policies to encourage remittances and then try to steer them towards productive investment purposes. It may be true that governments of recipient countries have been most likely to introduce policies that affect remitter behavior. This is partly because the governments in the host countries often view remittances as outflows of capital that could be productively put to use in their own country, and at the same time a burden in terms of transaction costs in return for little gain.

However, governments in donor countries do have something to gain from shaping remitter behavior and encouraging optimal use of remittances – if only in terms of increasing the formal transfer of remittances, improving transparency and data collection as a result, and reducing opportunities for illegal activities funded by or using remittances.

Governments of donor countries can also use active policies to direct remittances to productive purposes in some instances. They can, for example, go through aid agencies that are already operating in the receiving country, and understand the needs of the recipient country and its people. Aid agencies can work directly with remitters to help them understand how to use remittance services.

For example, both the UK's Department for International Development (DFID) and the United States Agency for International Development (USAID) have been involved in influencing how remittances are used in the countries that they are sent to. US foundations have done the same, as have a number of multilateral organizations including the World Bank and the International Labour Organization.

USAID has been particularly creative in working with the diaspora of different countries in the United States. Besides getting these immigrants to increase their remittance-based philanthropy, USAID workers have also convinced some migrants to return to their home countries on a volunteer basis to share the expertise they have acquired in the US. This has happened, in recent years, with both native-born Iraqis and Sudanese.

USAID workers have also encouraged immigrants from other countries to invest in aspects of their home economies that would be too risky to attract foreign direct-investment dollars. Additionally, they have adopted a diplomatic role, facilitating dialogue between the increasingly influential remittance-making immigrant groups in the US and the politicians and policymakers back home who want their support.

TAKING NOTICE

If there was ever a time when remittances could be ignored by government policy makers, that time has passed. Remittances are too big a part of international money flows for that, too tied into international politics, too important in terms of their upside potential and downside risks. This is simply not an area that will take care of itself.

Even the most basic remittance transactions – a transplanted family member sending money home to relatives – deserve a government's attention, if for no other reason than to make sure those transactions are safe, simple, and as low cost as possible. For most governments, however, the greatest potential lies in getting migrants to commit more of their remittance dollars to investments that go beyond immediate consumption. Because remittances involve a type of commitment that goes beyond pure self-interest, they are a remarkably stable source of financing in every economic climate. Recipient countries understand this and have built policies around remittances. Most donor countries, by contrast, are just waking up to the fact that they could have a role in increasing the productive impact of remittances. Donor or recipient, it's time for governments everywhere to treat these vast money flows strategically.

10
A remittances roadmap

Any country looking to establish an effective remittance policy needs to follow a clearly defined process, while engaging the necessary stakeholders and answering some key questions. The process of formulating a remittances strategy breaks down into four stages.

SET OBJECTIVES

The first task is to identify the purpose of the remittance strategy. The government has a number of options. It might simply choose to facilitate the movement of remittances, making it easier for migrants to send money and for family members to receive it. It might go further and also influence remitters' behaviors, including to whom or what they contribute money. It could focus on increasing the size of remittance flows, make them more formal, and ensure that they are well targeted. Another possibility would be to consider shifting the emphasis from consumption to investment.

GOVERNANCE MODELS

The next task is to establish a governance model. Once it settles on a strategy objective, the government (or its aid agency if it chooses to assign overall responsibility for its remittance strategy), needs to assign roles and responsibilities for achieving those strategy objectives. Engaging a range of stakeholders is essential.

In donor countries the remittance ecosystem includes aid agencies, central banks, banks, and other operators as well as home associations, and in many cases immigration entities are also involved. The role of government here is to ensure that the financial services sector is well regulated and that banks and other operators make the process of making remittances easier and more effective, minimizing the use of informal channels.

Both home associations and aid agencies can work on pooling resources and promoting collective remittances – contributions from groups of migrants instead of from individual migrants – which can be channeled towards development-oriented projects in the remitters' countries of origin, or used to help top up remittances. They can also help to educate remitters.

Labor and immigration entities, for their part, can help by working on initiatives with banks in the home countries of migrants in order to provide migrants with reliable low-cost loans, and facilitate their taking up a job in the host country. This can help to avoid migrants becoming dependent on unscrupulous creditors. Central banks and financial regulators can help to lower the cost of money transfers and minimize the incidence of illegal transfers.

In the recipient country, a number of different entities – including the banks and other operators, central banks, local governments, and development agencies – could advertise programs for remitters. NGOs and Civil Society Organizations also have a role to play in educating the recipients of remittances, creating awareness about the different options for sending remittances, and providing advice about using remittances more productively.

In addition, governments may work with or facilitate technology-related companies, which may be able to help roll out easy-to-use services that facilitate money transfers, as well as microfinance networks that allow migrants to remit money efficiently even in very small amounts. At the same time, they may want to share and source data with multilateral organizations such as the World Bank — which has been instrumental in gathering data about remittances and researching their impact.

In all cases governments should focus efforts on making sure all the members of the remittance ecosystem are well coordinated and communicating with each other. There is even scope for entities in both host and home countries to work together.

POLICIES AND PROGRAMS

Thirdly, a concrete set of policies and programs must be developed to advance the objectives. An example of a concrete policy is the regulation of costs, while an example of a program is the use of matching funds as an incentive to spur remittances in certain areas.

But what kind of tactics should be used? On one end of the continuum are active policies that seek to influence what remitters do with their money. On the other end are passive policies that encourage remittances by making them simpler and cheaper, but that don't attempt to change remitters' behavior.

So policies may be passive or active. Example of passive policies include providing information and creating awareness about the formal remittance process; using legislation and regulation to make remitting easier, encouraging the use of formal channels, and increasing competition thus lowering costs; implementing other measures to facilitate the remittance process and reduce costs; introducing data collection measures; and fostering dialogue between sending and receiving countries.

Active policies include encouraging investment in the receiving country's capital markets — through diaspora bonds, for example, or by securitizing remittance flows; supporting migrant associations and promoting the pooling of remittances; introducing retail payment systems; supporting financial innovation that involves remittances; and providing technical assistance.

While many of the policies are driven by the recipient country, donor countries also have a role to play here. They can, for example, use active policies to direct remittances to productive purposes in some instances. It is also possible to scale the diaspora money by matching remittances directly through government aid agencies, thus coupling aid with remittances.

MONITORING

Finally comes monitoring the effectiveness of those programs. This involves the development of agreed-on indicators to help the government assess whether its strategy objectives are being met. More importantly, though, it means that governments must find ways to collect data on remittances, in order to identify areas that need their attention, and monitor and assess the effectiveness of their interventions.

Should the government take a formal monitoring approach based on key performance indicators, or should it be more informal about the process, monitoring remittance flows on an ad hoc basis? If the level of data is limited, an ad hoc approach may be the government's only option.

Part III

Philanthropy for impact

Of the three financial forces that are the focus of *The Giving World*, philanthropy is perhaps undergoing the biggest changes of all.

In a twenty-first century context people tend to equate philanthropy with private giving, often on a grand scale, and invariably see it as altruistic in nature. They might have read about Microsoft founder Bill Gates and the Bill & Melinda Gates Foundation, or of mobile communications entrepreneur Mo Ibrahim and the Mo Ibrahim Foundation. They might be aware of the large sums of money pledged by members of royal families around the world, such as H.H. General Sheikh Mohammed bin Zayed Al-Nahyan, Crown Prince of Abu Dhabi, and H.S.H. Prince Albert II of Monaco.

But the reality is that philanthropic engagement stretches far beyond the handful of billionaires and high-profile donations which feature regularly in the mass media. A huge amount of resources is donated annually to philanthropic causes by a diverse range of individuals and organizations around the world. Despite being difficult to obtain, what data is available shows that in 2011 'at least 300 US foundations contributed over $770 million towards MDG Goal 1 of eradicating extreme poverty and hunger.'[95] And this is likely to increase in the future following the intergenerational transfer of wealth, (even accounting for the recent financial crisis), of some $58.1 trillion during the 55-year period from 2007–2061.[96]

This part of the book examines the different types of philanthropists, their motivations, and the mechanisms and channels through which they operate, and how these are changing. The latest trends are covered, including the rise of non-traditional forms such as venture philanthropy, social impact philanthropy, and 'philanthropeneurship'. The digital revolution and technological advancements, such as the development of crowdfunding and crowdsourcing, have also allowed for the wider spread of philanthropy, both in terms of reach and scale. Types of intermediaries and outcomes that could be targeted are discussed, as are some of the challenges that the philanthropic sector faces.

Despite the private nature of philanthropic decision making, governments can play an important role in helping philanthropists achieve their goals, while also serving societies' ends more generally by making philanthropy more development-oriented and widespread.

The role of governments as philanthropists has received very little, if any, attention. However, it is possible to view philanthropy as the discretionary allocation of wealth towards the wellbeing of communities that extend beyond the donor's family. If we set aside the notion that philanthropists must necessarily be private entities it becomes clear that governments can engage in philanthropy if their leaders allocate resources to philanthropic causes, from within or outside of their central budgets.

They can, for example, through structured financing, encourage the funding of large projects, providing relatively small amounts of grant financing which is topped up by philanthropists and private providers. Thus, by adopting a more engaged approach, governments have a unique ability to effect direct change through philanthropy.

There are also potential risks. The government's participation might crowd out the philanthropic contributions of non-governmental philanthropists, for example.

Whatever their level of involvement, there is much that governments can do. As explained in Chapter 14, there is considerable potential for governments to make a substantial impact as information providers, regulators, co-financers, and capacity builders. The following chapters outline how governments can engage more closely with the philanthropic world. They detail how governments might create a well-designed strategy to enhance the policy environment and incentivize the use of more effective channels for philanthropy.

11
The philanthropists

The word philanthropy derives from Hellenistic culture and the Ancient Greeks. It means a love of humans, of mankind, with those acts and ideas that enhance and nourish humanity being philanthropic acts. Today the philanthropy ecosystem stretches across the globe, far beyond Greece and Europe, and there are philanthropists on most continents and in most countries. Their motives for giving vary, but they are united by a desire to make people's lives better.

TYPES OF FUNDERS

Although the nature of philanthropic engagement varies across boundaries, societies, and organizations, it is possible to identify several trends among different types of philanthropists. If policymakers have a good understanding of the various types of funders that operate in a particular country it will help them with any efforts to influence philanthropic behavior within that country. To start with it is useful to distinguish between two types of funders: individuals and organizations.

Individuals

Many millions of individuals or individual households worldwide make philanthropic contributions. Typically, individual contributions make up the vast majority of philanthropic giving. This is clear from the 2012 Giving Report which states that 72 percent of all private donations in 2011 in the US were from individual sources. Of the rest, 14 percent were by foundations, 8 percent by bequests, with just 5 percent coming from corporations.

The patterns of giving by philanthropists vary widely based on a number of individual characteristics, most notably gender, age, household composition, and the level of education.

For example, at an international level, evidence suggests that a larger share of women engage in philanthropy than men. The World Giving Report 2014 reveals that a higher proportion of women than men gave money over the three-year period of 2010 to 2013, with a consistent differential of 0.8 percentage points.

This disparity is evident in the developed economies where women are more likely to donate money than men; 43.7 percent of women donated money, compared with 36.7 percent of men. However, in transitioning and developing economies men are slightly more likely than women to give. In 2010 the World Giving Index identified gender disparities across different regions. The region with the highest gender difference in giving was Australasia, where approximately 75 percent of surveyed females and 65 percent of surveyed males reported making philanthropic contributions in the previous year. Contrary to this aggregate trend, there were three regions in the world in which males gave marginally more than females: the Middle East (34 percent compared to 33 percent, relatively), North Africa (31 percent compared to 30 percent, respectively), and South Asia. Perhaps this discrepancy can be attributed to the specific family dynamics in these regions; men tend to be main income earners, or at least the largest income earners in the case of two working parents.

Interestingly, the gender difference persists beyond the extent of engagement in philanthropy. It is also evident in the approach to philanthropy.

Women have been found to do greater due diligence into philanthropic causes before deciding to support a particular one. They are also more likely to support initiatives that they believe will have a substantial impact – such as a community center, for example – rather than specific initiatives to which they have a personal affiliation.

Other gender differences related to philanthropy include women's desire for less public recognition for their contributions than their male counterparts, and greater commitment to their causes in the long run.[97] While these overall differences between the two genders persist, specific differences in behaviors may evolve over time, and there is evidence that younger males are increasingly engaging in philanthropic behaviors more typical of females.

Age can also make a difference. There is evidence that both the amount and types of giving may differ based on the age of philanthropists. If true, this is a significant finding. Large philanthropic donations tended to be associated with older donors. However, it is likely that business fortunes made by young entrepreneurs in their twenties and thirties from internet-related businesses will have more of an impact on philanthropic giving in the future.

The general global trend is that philanthropic contributions increase with age (although this is changing fast with the emergence of young high-net-worth individuals). According to the Wealth-X and Arton Capital philanthropy report 2014, for example, just 2.3 percent of ultra high-net-worth individuals were under 40, while some 60 percent were over 60, including 12.6 percent over 80.[98]

The types of causes that individuals support and the motivations that drive them to act philanthropically also appear to vary with age. One possible reason for this difference is that people are generally more established in their careers as they grow older. The drivers for giving are also likely to change with age, as well as the types of causes that appeal to or interest donors.

Certainly the 2014 World Giving figures show that, although the proportion of people giving aged over 50 has remained constant, the percentage of younger people donating is down, with the age group of 15 to 29 declining the most. One reason for this, suggests the World Giving Report, is the high levels of unemployment among young people globally.

Two other factors that appear to affect philanthropic giving are education and household composition. For example, American households with higher levels of education and similar levels of income are more likely to make philanthropic donations than households with lower levels of education.[99] [100] A possible plausible explanation is that as people attain a higher level of education they have more exposure to and a greater awareness and knowledge of some of the most significant issues that the world is facing, such as global poverty, humanitarian crises, climate change, and so on.

The relationship between wealth and philanthropic giving is far from straightforward. Evidence from the US suggests that, on average, increased wealth is associated with increased amounts of philanthropy, in absolute terms. Donations from households that have more than a million dollars of income (approximately 7 percent of the US population) constitute half of annual donations.[101]

The distribution of donations is interesting. For example, the share of income donated by individuals and households at the bottom of the income distribution is high, on average (approximately 4.6 percent in 2000). Then the share decreases until households have an income above $100,000, on average, at which point it increases again.[102] One explanation for this relatively high share of giving by low-income households may be the relatively higher membership of these households in religious groups – which usually advocate higher levels of giving.

Data on philanthropists, such as the total amount that they give annually and the amount that they give as a percentage of the founder's net worth, is rare and patchy at best. While some data does exist for US philanthropists and their foundations, it is difficult to obtain for philanthropists in other parts of the world.

Certainly, if you look at Asia the evidence suggests that philanthropy appears to be rising rapidly as economies develop and the wealth of individuals increases. Data from a variety of sources suggests that, from 2008 to

2010 inclusive, for example, philanthropic giving increased by 4.6 percent. In India, though, philanthropic donations were up by 429 percent. In China the percentage increase was 253 percent.

While no comprehensive data exists on philanthropic giving across the whole of Asia, the available evidence suggests that donations are significantly lower than in the West, and particularly in the US. However, this is changing. The data appears to show that the rate of increase in philanthropic giving is greater in Asia, a fact almost certainly linked to the increasing wealth in the region, which is now home to more than 4.3 million high-net-worth individuals (HNWIs).[103] The wealth of HNWIs in Asia grew to $14.2 trillion, up 18 percent. At the same time, the population of HNWIs was up 17 percent.[104]

If we take data from a number of sources and assemble a snapshot of some influential and generous Asian donors in 2014, it shows that Asian philanthropists gave to a wide variety of causes. In China, Chen Feng, chairman of the HNA Group, gave $1.6 million to the UN World Food Program (WPF) to help provide take-home rations under the WPF's school meals program in Ghana.

Dato Sri Tahir, the Indonesian founder and chairman of the Mayapada Group, pledged $100 million towards a health fund that aims to combat HIV, polio, malaria, and other diseases. In addition, he is spearheading a fundraising drive to persuade other wealthy individuals to donate to the Indonesia Health Fund. Elsewhere, Enrique Razon Jr. from the Philippines has donated considerable sums to reconstruction and relief efforts in the Philippines following Typhoon Haiyan.[105]

For the 2008 to 2010 period, for every thousand additional wealthy people, an extra $149 million in philanthropy was disbursed. In China the figure was an extra $5.5 million in philanthropy for every thousand additional wealthy people. But in the more developed markets of Singapore it led to an additional $0.92 million, while in US and Europe, where the markets are much more mature with a well-established base of high-net-worth individuals, the additional boost in giving from every thousand additional wealthy people was much less.

Of course, philanthropists can ensure that their philanthropic legacy extends long beyond their lifetime. Many very wealthy individuals do this through the establishment of foundations, and there is more detail about foundations, whether linked to organizations or private individuals, later.

Organizations

There are many different types of organizations associated with philanthropic funding. Three types of organization, in particular, are more closely associated with philanthropic activities. These are corporations, foundations (which can be started either by companies or by high-net-worth individuals), and governments.

When companies get involved in making philanthropic donations their contributions are often channeled via Corporate Social Responsibility (CSR) departments within their companies or, alternatively, through foundations that are affiliated with their companies. There has been some debate about whether corporate contributions should be considered philanthropy or purely CSR.

The argument is that because corporations often give to satisfy their own interests – to improve their reputations or expand their markets, for example – then this giving is not philanthropic. This would interpret philanthropy narrowly, as precluding contributions that are given for the benefit of the donor, which is a distinction that is difficult to make when looking at the whole range of types of donor and their motives for giving.

Most people think of governments as providers of public services, and of ODA, rather than philanthropists. This is because of the common conception of philanthropy as donations provided by private entities. On this basis the relationship between government and philanthropy would be limited to the regulation of the philanthropic sector or as a provider of information about that sector.

However, it is possible for governments to engage directly in philanthropy in those instances where they are donating resources that are not earmarked in their central budgets. For example, some government grants channeled to philanthropic organizations can be considered forms of government philanthropy. Governments can also take action to enhance the philanthropic capacity in the countries they govern at both a community and individual level. There are also examples of rulers of countries donating resources and these contributions are usually considered philanthropic, especially when the rulers use their private funds (where the distinction is often not as clear). Such philanthropic behavior can be observed in the donations of royal families to foundations and other philanthropic intermediaries, something that is common in some Middle East countries, for example.

Foundations are another important type of stakeholder in the world of philanthropy and an increasingly key player in international development. While their precise legal basis and structure may differ from country to country, essentially they are organizations typically funded by a wealthy individual or family and, at time, by corporations (e.g. the BMW foundation). The fund, then administered by trustees, is increased through investment, and used to finance projects that reflect the interest of the original founder (this may be determined by the trustees if the founder is no longer alive).

There are many hundreds of foundations across the world, representing billions of dollars of giving. Examples include the Wellcome Trust founded in 1936 by US-British pharmaceutical entrepreneur Henry Wellcome; the William and Flora Hewlett Foundation founded in the same year by Hewlett-Packard co-founder William Hewlett and his wife; the Swales Foundation founded by Indian media mogul Rohinton Screwvala; and the SOHO Foundation, co-founded in 2005 by Chinese nationals Pan Shiyi and Zhang Xin.

Not all foundations are established by individuals and their families. Some are set up by corporations, for example. A good example is the MasterCard Foundation, founded in 2006 through a gift of MasterCard Worldwide shares at the time the company was publically listed. This is increasingly becoming a trend especially in the case of large companies that want to formalize their philanthropic donations beyond their CSR programs.

Unlike individuals, the relationship between philanthropy and organizational wealth is more ambiguous. It depends in part on organization-specific rules that cover areas such as annual philanthropic disbursements and endowment size. For instance, in 2009 the Council Encouraging Corporate Philanthropy conducted a survey of 171 corporations and their philanthropic giving behavior. While there was an increase in aggregate giving in 2009, there was no consistent pattern of increases in the total average revenues leading to this increase in corporate philanthropy. It is very likely that the amount and type of philanthropy varies by sector or industry.

PREFERENCES AND MOTIVATIONS

The reasons for engaging in philanthropic activity vary widely. The decision about what causes people to give their support is strongly influenced by the motives and personal preferences of philanthropists and these differ between and across philanthropic individuals and groups.

At the individual level, motives range from religious obligation, to a sense of responsibility towards the local community, to a desire to make the world a better place. Thus commonly cited motives tend to fall into three categories: altruistic giving motivated simply by a desire to help those in perceived need; religious giving, motivated by the desire to further the work conducted by a particular church, and which might include contributions such as the payment of tithes, or zakat, an Islamic form of alms giving; and identity-associated giving, where the donor is motivated by a wish to help a specific group of recipients, who may share ethnicity, cultural background, or views on particular issues, for example.

Individuals may be influenced to varying degrees by one or more of these types of motives. There is also evidence to suggest that certain types of motives are more predominantly associated with particular groups of individuals.

The motivations of individual philanthropists will also influence the aims of any foundations that they might set up, and the direction of that Foundation under the trustees beyond their lifetime. Take one of the best-known foundations, the Bill and Melinda Gates Foundation, set up in

2000 by Bill Gates, founder of Microsoft, and his wife, Melinda. One of the world's largest transparently operated private foundations, its aims reflect the interests and passions of the Gates family, notably the desire to globally enhance healthcare, reduce extreme poverty, and expand educational opportunities and access to information technology.

Corporations have a different set of drivers from individuals. Generally they are driven by the overarching missions of their shareholders, the constituents that support them, plus the beneficiaries that organization's philanthropy is designed to support.

They may be driven by multiple motives at the same time. For example, there may be a desire to contribute to certain communities out of a sense of social responsibility, but at the same time the organization may hope to improve its reputation. In the case of for-profit entities this may lead to service provision that improves the image of the venture, or the market it taps into, for the joint benefit of shareholders and beneficiaries.

Individual and organizational preferences influence several aspects of philanthropic giving. For example, philanthropists may prefer to give to causes at home or internationally, or to individuals or larger groups of beneficiaries. They may prefer to support causes related to business sectors or geographical regions with which they have a personal or organizational connection. For example, diaspora groups may choose to support initiatives in their countries of origin, also known as collective remittances (see page 95).[106]

At the individual level, there is evidence that men are more inclined to support causes with which they have a direct connection, for instance, community centers they attended in their youth.[107]

Different donor preferences can contribute to the immense variation in philanthropic flows to different sectors and causes. For instance, in 2009 US philanthropic contributions to religious organizations were more than double those for educational purposes, at $100.95 billion compared to $40.01 billion, and more than 15 times the amount contributed to environmental causes, which was just $6.6 billion.[108]

12
How philanthropy works

The total amount contributed by philanthropists each year is considerable. This is certain. But it is hard to understand the true size and impact of philanthropic flows given the lack of reliable data. Aggregate estimates of philanthropic activities at national or regional levels are difficult to obtain.

This is partly because of the many different forms that philanthropic flows and activities can assume, and also because there is no central clearing house for philanthropic contributions through which these transfers can be tracked. It is also worth noting that a broadly accepted official definition of philanthropy remains elusive. This makes it difficult to establish which transfers should be measured. There are separate estimates for aggregate philanthropic financial flows, but these are drawn from a limited number of countries which have initiatives to enhance their philanthropic sectors. These estimates differ widely. Even rough estimates for countries outside the OECD's Development Assistance Committee are rare. Nevertheless, a quick look at estimates of annual philanthropic flows from the Muslim world, which range between $260 billion and $1 trillion a year, provides an indication of the huge values involved.

The US is one country where good data and visibility is available on philanthropic activities. Take the data from Giving USA, which publishes an annual report of the state of US charitable giving. Its 2015 report stated that Americans donated $358.38 billion to charity in 2014, with the highest proportion coming from individuals (72 percent).

Certainly, the evidence suggests that, in a number of countries, internationally oriented philanthropic donations are close to ODA contributions. Back in 2009, for example, a conservative estimate of international philanthropic flows originating in the US was approximately $37.5 billion, while US ODA for the same year was $28.8 billion. More recently, though, the emphasis has shifted slightly with US Giving's estimate of US philanthropic contributions to international affairs at $15.10 billion, while the OECD estimated that US ODA was $32.73 billion.

Data from the Hudson Institute collected between 2005 and 2010 shows the respective growth trends for remittances, ODA, and philanthropy. For philanthropic transactions from 2004 onwards the Hudson Institute uses data from the Center for Global Philanthropy (CGP) as its source, with OECD data used for the period before that. The data shows that in the space of two decades remittances have moved from second to first place in terms of aggregate amount transferred, reflecting an increase in global migration. In 20 years aggregated remittances have steadily increased in value from just below $50 billion to $174 billion. ODA, meanwhile, has stayed within a relatively narrow range, starting at close to $90 billion, falling away to almost touch $50 billion in 2000, before climbing to hit $120 billion in 2009.

For the majority of the 20-year period, however, philanthropic flows have barely broken through the $10 billion mark. But from 2000 they have grown steadily at a similar rate to both ODA and remittances, but remain someway behind both the others in amount at $52.5 billion.

Another measure that looks at philanthropic flows is the World Giving Index (WGI), the largest study into charitable behavior across the globe. The report is published annually by the Charities Aid Foundation, using data from Gallup's Worldview World Poll which looks at three variables and measures giving behavior – giving money, volunteering time, and helping a stranger. The 2014 WGI report was the fifth edition of the WGI and contained giving data covering 2009 to 2013 from 135 countries.

Interestingly, the US is the only country that is ranked in the top ten across all three giving behaviors. This helps to secure its position as the number one country in the overall WGI, alongside Myanmar. Though some might be surprised at Myanmar's elevated position in the ranking, it is less surprising if you consider that 90 percent of the population follows the Theravada school of Buddhism which advocates the charitable giving of money to support, among other things, the living costs of ordained monks and nuns.[109]

What is also clear from the WGI ranking is that the countries with a high WGI position are not necessarily those with the highest GDP. And, as the report stresses, membership of the G20 is not a prerequisite for a high-ranking position either. Thus Trinidad and Tobago, Bhutan, Sri Lanka, Malta, Iran, and Jamaica are all in the top 20 countries. Overall the top ten countries are: Myanmar (joint #1), United States of America joint #1), Canada, Ireland, New Zealand, Australia, Malaysia (joint #7), United Kingdom (joint #7), Sri Lanka, and Trinidad and Tobago.[110]

With respect to the three measures, the US, Iraq, Trinidad and Tobago, Jamaica, and Liberia make up the top five countries for helping a stranger. Myanmar, Malta, Thailand, Ireland, and the UK make up the top five countries for donating money. While in terms of volunteering time Turkmenistan, Myanmar, Sri Lanka, and Uzbekistan are the top four countries – Canada, New Zealand, Tajikistan, and the US tie for fifth place.

Despite the lack of clarity on its actual size, philanthropy remains largely impactful. Whatever the breakdown in terms of amounts given and regional differences, to understand how that money can really make a difference a number of elements in between philanthropist and outcome need to be considered. These include the form the philanthropic contribution takes, the outcome targeted, the channels used, and the financial methods used to transfer wealth.

FORMS AND OUTCOMES

Philanthropic contributions can take a number of forms and be directed at several different types of outcome.

As far as forms go, financial giving is probably the form most associated with philanthropic acts. However, contributions can also be gifts in kind, such as clothing and equipment, for example. A third kind of philanthropic contribution is human capital, and this would include labor and technical expertise.

As well as taking a variety of forms, philanthropic contributions can also be targeted towards three main types of outcome: developmental, humanitarian, and/or charitable.

Developmental outcomes are the result of philanthropic programs and projects aimed at improving the quality of life, reducing poverty, and addressing socio-economic challenges. They might include, for example, the construction of roads, hospitals, and schools. It includes the Carter Center's (set up by Jimmy and Rosalynn Carter) work on health, such as its attempts to eradicate the guinea worm or control bilharziasis ('snail fever'), and the Joseph Rowntree Foundation's social policy research.

Often the funding is targeted at gaps in existing development aid programs, whether that is due to cutbacks following the financial crisis or ideological policy reasons. According to the UNDP, for example, some 300 US foundations contributed more than $770 million towards the first Millennium Development Goal of eradicating extreme poverty and hunger.

Humanitarian outcomes, on the other hand, result from philanthropic assistance designed to save lives, alleviate suffering, and protect human dignity, especially in cases of natural disasters. An example of a humanitarian outcome would be assistance given to refugees and displaced persons. Take the Global Citizen Foundation's Amal project in Jordan's refugee camp, for example ('amal' means 'hope' in Arabic). The project, a collaboration with the nonprofit ASmallWorld Foundation, was initiated by Dubai-based fashion brand GlamOnYou and aims to provide recreational facilities for children in the refugee camps set up as consequence of the war in Syria. It is currently in the Zaatari Camp in Jordan, the second biggest refugee camp in the region.[111]

The Red Cross includes a donate button on its website allowing people to direct their charitable giving towards humanitarian causes. Similarly, iTunes initiated a global relief effort in partnership with Facebook to help support communities affected by typhoon Haiyan.

Then there are charity outcomes that result from philanthropy related to cultural or religious purposes. Many religions have a long tradition of encouraging charitable giving, from the Russian Orthodox to the Catholic churches, from Judaism to Islam, Hinduism to Buddhism. For followers of Islam this might include building mosques, facilitating hajj trips, and distributing food during the holy month of Ramadan. In the West, giving associated with religion has been declining in recent years.

On the cultural side, philanthropic giving has been increasing. In the US, for example, of an estimated total of $358.38 billion given to charity in 2014, a record $17.23 billion was directed at arts, culture, and the humanities.

One of the distinctive features that distinguishes philanthropy from other major forms of transfer of income is that contributions can be directed towards causes in the home country or, as is increasingly the case, they can be used for the benefit of international causes. Both official development assistance and remittances are typically transferred to beneficiaries in other countries. In contrast, a significant proportion of philanthropic giving has traditionally been directed towards the home country.

These transfers also differ from a fourth category of international flows, foreign direct investment (FDI), because of the different purpose of the flows. Unlike ODA, remittances and philanthropic flows, FDI is provided as an investment with the primary goal of maximizing financial returns. However, this does not mean that philanthropists do not seek to measure the impact of their philanthropic endeavors. As they strive to do this, terms similar to those used in financial metrics – such as return on mission or return on social impact – are becoming more common.

CHANNELS FOR PHILANTHROPIC FLOWS

Philanthropists have many different channels available through which they can make their donations. The channels, which make up the institutional landscape of philanthropy, include foundations, NGOs, faith-based organizations (FBOs), and online marketplaces that match philanthropists to causes. They also include multilaterals. People can contribute to humanitarian relief plans via UNHCR, for example, in the same way that they can through many NGOs or faith-based organizations.

The types of channels philanthropists choose to use depend in large part on factors such as the nature of the channels available to them, their awareness of those channels, the amount or size of the intended donation, preferences about the amount of intermediation involved in their philanthropic engagements, or about the level of control over the administration of their donations.

Through the use of these channels philanthropists are able to match the activities that they want to engage in, and the type of philanthropy they want to practice, with the existing opportunities available.

Philanthropists can choose to provide resources for specific projects, while stipulating minimal or no requirements for the measurement of any outcomes. Or they may prefer to offer their support via an outcome or output-based program that links the resources it expends to some method of measuring progress. The different approaches that are available can, to varying degrees, incentivize outcome orientations in the use of philanthropic resources.

Customarily these intermediaries accept contributions from philanthropists and use those resources to advance specific philanthropic causes. Some offer specific programming and disburse funding to organizations and individuals through grants. Others may be more operational in nature. In this case they will use the philanthropic resources channeled through them to administer programs. These might include, for example, primary education programs in developing countries, or workforce development programs in an urban settlement.

Philanthropic intermediaries may focus on supporting individuals and causes where the additional return on every dollar donated is comparatively small. Alternatively, they may wish to direct their efforts towards high-return philanthropic investments.

Because of the significant size of their individual donations large-scale, high-wealth donors are able to give their funds directly to beneficiaries. Some prominent philanthropists, such as Bill Gates, engage in direct philanthropy initially, transferring resources directly to their intended beneficiaries. This is often the route taken when philanthropists prefer to retain complete control over their giving, are not aware of, or do not have access to other channels.

When contributions are directly transferred to beneficiaries, philanthropists have complete control over the administration of their contributions, such as identification of beneficiaries. Another benefit is that recipients receive the entire donation as there are no administrative costs associated with direct giving.

Philanthropists may look for ways to make larger, systemic impacts.[112] Small-scale donors may choose to band together and pool their resources so they can achieve the maximum impact possible. At the same time this usually means that they are locked into choosing channels with a high degree of intermediation and thus have less control over their donations.

Rather than giving directly, philanthropists can choose channels such as internet-based platforms, giving circles, foundations, CSR departments, or hometown associations. There are an increasing number of alternative channels available. As we will see in the next chapter, technology enables the creation and spread of online marketplaces that allow philanthropists to select the beneficiaries of their resources directly and, to varying degrees, directly channel their resources to them. These include platforms such as the internet-based campaigning platform Causes, Razoo, and online crowdfunding money-raising websites.

The organizational structure of the intermediaries and the approaches that they use to transfer funding will have a strong bearing on the types and magnitudes of the outcomes achieved. Operational factors that could have an effect on those outcomes, for example, include the amount of overheads that these organizations require, which determines the share of donated resources that reach the intended beneficiaries. It also includes the mandates that they have which dictate whether and how they can operate, the strategies that they employ to guide their activities, and the knowledge and expertise of their staff.

It is also worth remembering that funding can be channeled through foundations from a number of different sources. The UN notes, for example, that there are foundations funded by endowments from individuals or particular families, through corporate endowments, by community fundraising, and also mixed funding, from all or some of individuals, companies, other foundations, even government agencies.[113]

In choosing this type of channel the philanthropists agree to relinquish a degree of control over the administration of their resources. Where the channel used is professionally managed, it may be that the philanthropist benefits from a streamlined administrative process, such as identifying and partnering with beneficiaries. This reduces transaction costs and increases efficiency. And there are times when grant-making philanthropic organizations choose to allocate philanthropic resources to governments to execute under-funded programs.

At the same time, the success and power of some philanthropic organizations means that they have also become channels for the flow of philanthropic funds. Governments are using foundations as a channel through which they send their foreign assistance for specific causes.

In general, large philanthropic organizations are increasingly collaborating with governments to resolve larger policy problems. The Carter Center is a good example of a philanthropic organization that works with governments to address many of the problems that the Center hopes to solve. For example, the Center – as noted, founded by former US President Jimmy Carter and his wife Rosalynn in partnership with Emory University – has led a coalition of organizations, government bodies, and other interested partners in reducing the incidence of Guinea worm disease.

FINANCING

The way that philanthropists contribute, and the impact of their contributions, is likely to vary depending on the way that funding is disbursed in the philanthropy value chain. Funding contributions vary enormously, from the small ad hoc cash payments by millions of givers to sizeable endowments from very wealthy individuals. Funding can be by grant or loan, with strings attached or otherwise.

Whatever the method, the type of funding and the transfer mechanism used often has a direct effect on the outcome of those contributions. It may do this, for example, through the way funding mechanisms are structured and through the incentives created for the recipients of those funds. The amount of control that the philanthropist has over the way a particular method of funding is used will vary, depending on the way that that funding distributed, and the conditions attached. Each type of funding has advantages and disadvantages.

Take the use of cash, for example, a relatively straightforward and easily accessible means of funding for most. Cash can be used to provide loans or grants. It is commonly used for widespread, ad hoc grants of relatively small amounts of money. However, these types of payments are not a guaranteed long-term source of funding, and are always at risk of drying up, depending on the factors affecting their donation, and disrupting capital-intensive projects that are long term in nature.

On the other hand, cash is particularly useful in fast-moving humanitarian situations. In these cases cash allows relief workers to use funding in a way which matches the needs on the ground at any particular moment. Equally, by acquiring relief products locally or regionally, charities can reduce shipping costs and deliver assistance more rapidly.

Alternatively, endowments start with having capital donated to an investment trust or fund, and then use the income generated from that capital and further capital donations as the source of philanthropic giving. Endowments tend to be longer term, running over many decades and, given their long-term nature, are typically preferred over cash for larger projects.

Whether it is many small cash payments or a few large endowments by bank transfer, funding may come with some conditions attached or be relatively unfettered.

Where philanthropists give pure grants, for example, there is no intention of gaining any recompense for the philanthropist. The direct grants may be provided directly to beneficiaries, either through foundations, CSR departments, or a variety of other means. A grant might be in the form of unconditional (also known as unrestricted) grants, and have no reporting requirements and be available for any type of general expenditure, including running costs. However, these types of grants may create weak incentives for beneficiaries to focus on and document the results they achieve. Alternatively, grant funding may be conditional (or restricted). This means that the funding has requirements attached, such as it must be directed at capital expenditure, for example, or at a specific cost item or project, or geographical region.

Then there are loans. Philanthropic loans are typically provided at concessional rates of interest or, at near zero percent. Loans are not always popular as they place a financial burden on the borrower and, unlike corporations, charities do not always have a regular income stream, which can make structuring loan payments more problematic. One the other hand, charities are seen as relatively high risk for conventional loans, and so at least philanthropic loans can provide funding if required. Loan obligations often bring with them the kind of financial discipline and reporting that is increasingly demanded of philanthropic activity.

Loans can be provided by organizations. A good example is the Charities Aid Foundation (CAF) in the UK, which is both an authorized bank and a registered charity. It provides a range of loan funding, with unsecured funding up to £500,000, typically for a maximum period of two to five years, while secured loans are available up to £5 million for periods of up to 25 years maximum.

Another innovative form of funding that has played a growing role in the philanthropic value chain is microfinance. The microfinance industry was pioneered by Nobel Laureate, and founder of the Grameen Bank, Muhammad Yunus. The idea is to make small loans available to poor people and communities, often targeting the women in these communities, in order to develop micro enterprises, build savings, and improve their standard of living and economic position. A good example of microfinance at work is the Hunger Project (http://thp.org) which facilitates the empowerment of women using microfinance in order to alleviate poverty and hunger.

Although not a typical form of philanthropy disbursement, loans at very concessional rates and aimed at charities could often be identified as such.

Modern technology is enabling philanthropic giving on a global scale. Giving via internet and mobile phone platforms, as well as loans targeted at social initiatives through similar channels, are becoming increasingly popular. It is part of the new wave of philanthropy that is described in more detail in the next chapter.

There are other methods of financing, as well. An individual or organization might lease an asset, such as a building or equipment, to an NGO, for example.

While philanthropists typically hope their contributions will make an impact, in many cases it can be a challenge to identify and measure the results achieved through their efforts. This happens for a number of reasons, including a lack of attention on the results; inadequate consensus on what the results should be, and how they should be achieved and measured; and the inherent challenges associated with measuring the results and attributing those results to specific interventions.

This is particularly important because small contributions can be wasted if they are directed towards causes where incremental support is not enough to bring about change. Instead the impact may be sub-optimal. Find the right cause, however, direct the same amount and type of contribution towards a different but more appropriate cause, one that fully meets the financial need of the beneficiary, and it can lead to a more positive impact. Take the likely results from the impact of a contribution of $100 to support an orphan in Dar es Salaam, Tanzania, versus the same contribution to support an orphan in Hong Kong. Where poverty is greater much more can be achieved with smaller sums of money.

But if the philanthropic approach is more results-based, and makes funding conditional on the recipient of the contributions achieving certain specified results, this creates much stronger incentives for the recipients to measure activities, communicate targets and achieve results.

13
Philanthropy 2.0 – the evolving value chain

There are many changes underway in the world of philanthropy. Not least in terms of the profile of philanthropists, the types of philanthropy, the expectations of philanthropists, and the impact of new technologies.

A NEW GENERATION OF PHILANTHROPISTS

Take the profile of philanthropists. In the past the archetypal philanthropist was someone who had spent the best part of a lifetime creating a business empire, that in turn created the wealth that allowed them to embark on their philanthropic endeavors. As a result most philanthropists came to philanthropy later in life. Today, however, there are increasing numbers of individuals making large amounts of money very early on in their careers.

Take the 2015 announcement by Facebook co-founder Mark Zuckerberg who, along with his partner Priscilla Chan, pledged to donate 99 percent of their Facebook shares to their philanthropic foundation, the Chan Zuckerberg Initiative. The value of the shares at the time was $45 billion. As befits the approach of the new generation of young philanthropists, Zuckerberg was 31 when he made the announcement after the birth of his first child. The Chan Zuckerberg Initiative is structured as a Limited Liability Company which allows Zuckerberg much greater flexibility over the way the money is used.

As Zuckerberg noted in a Facebook post at the time, the structure of the foundation 'enables us to pursue our mission by funding non-profit organizations, making private investments and participating in policy debates – in each case with the goal of generating a positive impact in areas of great need ... What's most important to us is the flexibility to give to the organizations that will do the best work – regardless of how they're structured.'[114]

At the time the Initiative's objectives were, 'to join people across the world to advance human potential and promote equality for all children in the next generation. Our initial areas of focus will be personalized learning, curing disease, connecting people, and building strong communities.'[115]

Zuckerberg's philanthropic gesture is sure to be followed by many other wealthy entrepreneurs of his generation. A 2014 report by *The Economist* on the subject identified three distinct types of young philanthropist: idealistic entrepreneurs, philanthropic financiers, and engaged heirs.[116]

The early access to wealth is typified by the tech boom and the spate of dot-com millionaires, many of whom have made fortunes by their mid-thirties. They then turn to philanthropy. In doing so, these young innovative philanthropists are applying some of the skills acquired and lessons learned in their careers as entrepreneurs to their philanthropy. One study, by NextGenDonors, reveals that the new wave of philanthropists is motivated by obtaining value and achieving impact, and they are highly engaged in doing so.

The indications are that the new generation of donors wants more visibility on where their donations are being used, and the outcomes. This was highlighted in an article in the *Financial Times* by Lucy Warwick-Ching, entitled 'UK charity donors demand transparency in return for cash'. In the article Alberto Lidji, chief executive of Maximum Philanthropic Benefit, a firm that advocates measuring philanthropic impact, noted 'Gone are the days when donors put their hands in their pockets without asking questions.' As the article also recounts, a number of clients of Coutts Bank who had set up charitable trusts were making visits to the recipients of their trust donations – whether that meant traveling to Rwanda or to a boxing gym – to see how their money was spent.

Indeed the changing nature of philanthropists is reflected in the rise of social entrepreneurship, a phenomenon that has been tracked and analyzed in many books devoted solely to that topic.

EMERGING MODELS

Alongside the emergence of a new generation of philanthropists new types of philanthropy are emerging, such as strategic philanthropy, venture philanthropy, and entrepreneurial philanthropy.

Consider venture philanthropy. Loosely defined, venture capital has been described by the OECD as being aimed at 'systems and sectors' rather than specific initiatives that have a very limited local impact. Initiatives that are likely to receive the attention of venture philanthropy include education and healthcare, supporting small businesses, and encouraging sustainable energy use. A typical example of venture philanthropy is the support of initiatives that are helping households in the developing world replace kerosene lamps with lower cost solar technology lamps.

With the rise of the new philanthropist comes a desire to assess the impact of their brand of philanthropy and hold the channels through which that philanthropy is exercised accountable. Greater transparency is sought. There is an emphasis on measuring impact with new metrics being used.

These include social return on investment, originally championed in the 1990s by REDF, a US venture philanthropy fund.[117] It is a measure that is even gaining support from some governments, as in the UK. With many of these new measures the intention is to focus on the outcomes and measuring the outcomes, rather than on the amounts of money raised or used per se. It is about the effectiveness of the deployed funds.

TECHNOLOGIES

New technologies are changing the face of philanthropy, supporting new and emerging trends in philanthropic giving. They help to maintain transparency on philanthropic performance. The use of online platforms allows widespread monitoring. At the same time these technologies allow initiatives with philanthropic support to scale up more easily, and in ways which make fundraising widespread and immediate. Take the comparatively recent social media campaign and internet meme of the ice-bucket challenge, which had celebrities pouring a bucket of ice over themselves, videoing it and posting the act online, and nominating others to do the same in the name of a charitable cause. This is a good example of harnessing the power of the internet to take a cause global, reaching millions, and raising millions.[118]

Another good example of how technology is transforming philanthropy is the use of the internet to channel giving, and also loans. Crowdfunding, for example, is a relatively new phenomenon made possible by the ubiquity of the internet. With crowdfunding people come together and collectively network and pool their money, usually via the internet, to support efforts initiated by other people or organizations. It can be used to make both loans and grants. While crowdfunding is used for a variety of different purposes it is a very convenient mechanism to enable people to donate money to specific causes and maximize their impact when doing so.

A variety of crowdfunding platforms have emerged to allow ordinary web users to support specific philanthropic projects without the need to donate large amounts of money. Take the web-based initiative Global Giving. It is the world's largest global crowdfunding community, founded by former World Bank executives Mari Kuraishi and Dennis Whittle in 2002. The platform allows individuals to browse through a portfolio of small-scale projects proposed by nonprofit organizations from around the world, and donate funds to projects of their choice. Since its launch, GlobalGiving has raised $193,929,255 from 486,681 donors who have supported 12,906 projects.[119] Kiva is another well-known web-based crowdfunding platform.

The crowdfunding phenomenon has been covered widely in the media, particularly regarding its ability to democratize philanthropy, once seen as the sole province of the very wealthy. According to crowdfunding industry research firm Massolution, crowdfunding platforms were estimated to have raised $16.2 billion worldwide in 2014. This new internet phenomenon has even given rise to #GivingTuesday, an online annual crowdfunding day.[120]

FINANCIAL INNOVATION

While technology has enabled conventional types of giving to be rolled out on a global scale, the involvement of a new generation of philanthropists has also given rise to novel forms of philanthropic financing.

Consider social impact bonds, an innovative form of investment tied to the outcomes of social initiatives. These bonds are based on a commitment from the government to use a proportion of the savings that result from improved social outcomes to reward the private investors who fund the early intervention activities. Reaching a particular target triggers a particular level of payment. For example, in the UK the Department of Justice ran a scheme across a number of years through the not-for-profit organization Social Finance: private investors funded third sector providers to help reduce the prisoner reoffending rate by at least 7.5 percent.

The British government has given a boost to social impact bonds in the UK by establishing the Centre for Social Impact Bonds in the Cabinet Office. The Centre supports the use and development of social impact bonds in a number of ways, including providing information and guidance on developing social impact bonds; detailing case studies; providing access to an online toolkit; disseminating the latest research and thought leadership on the topic; and funding some of the outcome payments for SIBs.

It is worth noting that while nominally titled 'bonds' they are often structured using special purpose vehicles and, given the variety of outcome metrics used, assessing the risks involved can be difficult. Also, although there has been support for social impact bonds in the UK, and they are beginning to gain traction elsewhere, their performance is mixed.

In the US, for example, a social impact bond that involved Goldman Sachs and Bloomberg Philanthropies aimed to reduce reoffending by teenage inmates at Rikers Island jail. However, the funded program made little difference to recidivism rates. On the other hand, from the perspective of solving social problems, while the SIB-funded program may not have paid off, it still allowed the authorities to test possible solutions to reduce reoffending.

Another example of how philanthropy is adopting increasingly sophisticated methods of financing is the use of structured financing. In order to encourage lending to NGOs, the debt can be structured in a way that allows philanthropists to guarantee the initial layer. In a loan of £1 million, for example, a philanthropist may underwrite the first £100,000. Providing a first loss cushion makes it more likely that other lenders will contribute the rest of the £1 million, and do so at lower rates of interest.[121]

For the philanthropist, while they do not gain any interest from providing the first layer, they do get their loan returned in full – assuming the recipient of the loan does not default, or partially default. This enables them to reuse the same money for a similar purpose. This differs from a grant where the philanthropist parts with the money.

Governments may also play a role in this type of structured financing arrangement. A government may, by way of grant or loan, provide the initial layer, with philanthropists participating at lower rates of return than other private investors.

A good example of a philanthropic loan guarantee scheme at work is the Schwab Charitable microfinance guarantee program, which was launched in 2008. Donors with a charitable gift account are able to set aside a portion of the money in their account to guarantee microfinance loans by the Grameen Bank to some of the world's poorest entrepreneurs. In this way donors get additional impact, as their funds can be used first as a guarantee and then also as a grant.[122]

Structured finance enabled a consortium of four charitable organizations in Australia to help save a number of childcare centers previously owned by ABC Learning, one of the world's biggest publicly quoted childcare providers which was at risk of going bust.

The firm was rescued from voluntary liquidation by The Goodstart Consortium, formed by Social Ventures Australia, the Benevolent Society, the Brotherhood of St Laurence, and Mission Australia. The Goodstart Consortium used layered financing, raising AUS$95 million in cash to buy ABC Learning's 678 childcare centers. It also raised an additional AUS$70 million to finance the day-to-day running of the new social venture. The syndicated loan included senior debt from the National Australia Bank, a layer of finance from the Australian government as a long-dated loan, and a further layer of finance from 41 social investors, foundations and individuals using a new financial instrument called a social capital note, with a rate of return of 12 percent.[123]

14
Proactive government

As already noted, although reliable global data is difficult to obtain, there is no question that total annual philanthropic giving adds up to a very large amount of money. It is money that already has significant beneficial impact. But there is still potential to achieve more, and governments can play a major role in enhancing the scope and effectiveness of philanthropy.

Philanthropy is primarily giving by private individuals or organizations. However, governments can have a significant and beneficial impact on philanthropy. While philanthropy should not be driven by governments, they can enable it, and enhance its effectiveness across the entire sector through targeted policymaking.

Specific policies and policy environments can incentivize, facilitate, or discourage philanthropic giving. Over time, the effect of these environments on the factors that influence philanthropy can lead to a difference in the size and impact of philanthropic sectors across countries.

Governments can act in order to increase the efficacy of philanthropic funding, both in terms of the amount donated and the strategic impact that this type of giving has. And, in many cases, governments are closely involved in philanthropic work. While the term 'non-governmental organization' suggests that NGOs are completely independent from government, the reality is often slightly different. Often NGOs receive a significant proportion of their funding from government. Similarly a large proportion of disaster response and management funding comes from governments. Even where the involvement is more distanced, they can play a very important role. To do so, though, policymakers need to understand how best to utilize the policy tools they have at their disposal in order to shape policy environments and so bring about the appropriate changes.

Policy tools that governments use to influence philanthropic giving, whether through policies that promote philanthropic giving or policies that boost strategic impact, can be divided into four groups: regulation, information, co-financing, and capacity building. Regulation and information are used to promote and affect the quantity of giving, while co-financing and capacity building are used to affect the results of philanthropy. Given that there is some overlap between the policy goals, proper utilization of government tools may well obtain the double benefits of both promoting increased giving as well as encouraging smarter giving.

Generally speaking philanthropy is slowly evolving from 'check book charity' to a more visionary and strategic approach which requires better policies to affect the direction and impact of philanthropic flows.

Governments, particularly in countries with more mature charity and philanthropic sectors, are increasingly turning their attention to co-financing and capacity building to pursue a more strategic approach to philanthropy. 'Smart' philanthropy places an important emphasis on innovation, scale, and measurable results in its execution, and aims to make a long-term impact on social issues. Consequently smart-philanthropist donors are those that are increasingly focused on specific goals, the effective use of resources, and the adequate measurement of the impacts of philanthropy.

Although there is a clear trend in philanthropy for a more strategic approach in some parts of the world, in regions like Asia the philanthropy sector is much more immature. It remains to be seen how long it will take for strategic philanthropy to become a widely accepted practice, or indeed whether it will ever be widely embraced and publicly disclosed.

REGULATION

Governments have used many different approaches to regulate and govern the philanthropic sector. These include registration and licensing, the accreditation of philanthropic organizations, and creating a supportive regulatory and tax environment.

One policy tool frequently used for promoting and encouraging activity within the philanthropy sector is regulation. When creating the best regulatory environment for philanthropy to flourish in, a critical challenge for governments is striking the appropriate balance between involvement that creates an environment and provides information that optimizes resources and implementation, and involvement that overburdens and constrains the sector. Both over- and under-regulation can create barriers to entry, whether through creating and adding to administrative burden at one extreme or removing the need for any oversight or accountability at the other.

Through regulations and active governance, governments can play a significant role in increasing the efficiency and transparency of the philanthropic sector, and thus in increasing financial flows. For example, inefficiency and a lack of transparency are often the result of poor practices in underdeveloped sectors, where the professional structures that would ensure organizations' accountability to donors have not yet been put in place.

Registration and licensing

Through registration and licensing of philanthropic bodies, along with continuous engagement and monitoring, governments can enforce a higher level of transparency in the sector. Accrediting philanthropic organizations and initiatives that excel in effective monitoring, good accounting practices, and organizational transparency will help to build a culture of trust in the sector, and encourage greater and more frequent participation.

Regulation as a policy tool is also used in contexts where governments want to restrict certain types of philanthropic flows, namely in cases where there are security concerns. Take, for example the case of Coutts and Co. in the UK. Popularly known as the Queen's bank, Coutts and

Co. is a private bank owned by the Royal Bank of Scotland Group, with a rich tradition of over 300 years of experience in banking and charity services. In 2012, Coutts was fined £8.75 million by the Financial Services Authority (FSA) for failing to take adequate measures to prevent money laundering. At the time the FSA said the failings 'resulted in an unacceptable risk of Coutts handling the proceeds of crime.'[124] The bank responded by pointing out that there was no evidence that money laundering took place as a result of their deficient controls, although they recognized that their systems weren't totally adequate and have since taken steps to improve them.

In cases like this governments increase restrictions on charitable contributions, which has the effect of increasing the transaction costs associated with philanthropic giving. This can have a braking effect, reducing philanthropic flows and minimizing the risk of non-transparent funds. (In other cases tax reductions can be used to incentivize larger flows of philanthropy.)

Taxation

A common method of using regulation to promote philanthropic giving is by incentivizing philanthropic activities through tax benefits. Tax benefits exempt donors from paying certain income taxes as a reward and encouragement for their philanthropic contributions.

For instance, while approximately 65 to 85 percent of Americans are philanthropists, there are countries in Europe where philanthropy is equally widespread. However, giving in America is far more generous. On average, Americans give approximately twice as much per capita than the amount given by philanthropists in the most generous European countries.

These differences are widely attributed to the more generous tax benefits offered in the US, and the differences in government welfare provision between America and countries in the EU.[125] According to one survey by the Bank of America, for example, 67 percent of Americans would decrease their philanthropic giving if tax benefits were cut. This just reinforces how effective tax policies can be in promoting philanthropic giving.

Not only do tax benefits incentivize donations and the decision-making process in the creation of foundations and endowments, but they also send an important signal to society. They emphasize the public value of philanthropic acts.

A GENTLE NUDGE

Governments don't have to resort to the regulatory system to influence philanthropic giving. Another way that governments have been trying to influence the behavior of private individuals in order to benefit public policy objectives is through behavioral science. Around the world academics have investigated the way people behave, factors that affect that behavior, and therefore how governments can gently manipulate those factors to influence the behavior of their citizens. Nudging is about subtle influence, usually by providing additional choice, rather than prohibition or the reduction of choice. A commonly quoted example is putting nutritious food choices such as fruit at eye level in shops, restaurants, and cafeterias in order to encourage healthy eating (as opposed to banning stodgy and unhealthy foods).

Social initiatives designed to influence behavior in this way are known as nudges, while the field of study is known as nudge theory. The 2008 book *Nudge, Improving Decisions about Health, Wealth and Happiness* by academics Richard Thaler and Cass Sunstein, raised the profile of nudge theory, and attracted the attention of governments. In 2010 the UK coalition government was sufficiently persuaded of the concept's potential to introduce the Behavioral Insight Team (BIT), popularly known as the nudge unit, operating out of the Cabinet Office. The team has subsequently been partially privatized but is still in existence.

The process of developing nudge initiatives usually runs through a series of steps from identifying the behavior to be changed and the target population, to designing the behavioral change intervention, then running the initiative and evaluating its success. One of the big benefits of adopting a nudge approach is the potential to achieve behavioral change, without coercion, at relatively low cost.

So with philanthropy, for example, there are several ways in which government can nudge the different parties involved to influence behavior. Indeed the UK's nudge unit has, in conjunction with the Charities Aid Foundation, trialed a number of initiatives and written up the resulting insights in a report 'Applying behavioral insights to charitable giving.'[126]

The report reveals four behavioral insights derived from the academic literature on altruism and giving, which were then trialed by the BIT. The first insight is to make giving easy. This might include providing the option to increase future payments, and automatically enrolling senior staff into giving schemes with an opt-out available, rather than the other way around.

Another insight is to 'attract attention' and make charitable giving more attractive to donors. This might mean using personalized messages, for example, or rewarding desired behavior through fund matching.

The third insight is about focusing on the social, trying to encourage giving by altering people's perception of it, and making giving a social norm. Initiatives here could include using famous people to socially legitimize giving, raising the profile of giving within social groups to maximize peer effects, and establish group norms around giving.

The fourth insight offered by the BIT and CAF report concerned timing. The report suggested that 'timing matters' and that with the right timing it was possible to increase donations. One timing initiative is to ensure charitable appeals are made at the times most likely to produce donations; in December, rather than January, for example.

INFORMATION

The availability of relevant information plays a big role in promoting philanthropic activity. Governments can introduce policies or take other measures that play a role in increasing the availability of this information. Obviously this is particularly important if the information does not exist already or is difficult to access. Specific data that is relevant includes data on sector performance, information on the types of causes that people can support, the channels that they can use, and the potential impact that their support may help achieve. All of this data has the potential to alter the decisions that are taken by philanthropists.

The information that governments are most likely to be concerned with can be categorized into three groups. Each category targets a different audience depending on the level of involvement in the sector.

Knowledge, awareness, and data

The first category of information is knowledge and data which aims to make people more aware of and informed about the local philanthropic sector. It is targeted at those people who are not yet involved in the sector.[127] This type of information might, for example, introduce people to the concept of philanthropy, and provide details on the types of philanthropic flows, the number and kinds of organizations, the activities involved, and the size of the sector.

Information of this type can be channeled to the public in the form of awareness campaigns through various information platforms. The global digital revolution means that governments can use web-based platforms and databases to help both the public and government employee and representatives find philanthropic data easily.

It is possible for governments to act as advocates for philanthropy. This is something, for example, that the provincial government in Alberta, Canada, does particularly effectively with its Alberta's Promise initiative. The initiative, detailed on its website, www.albertaspromise.org, is a partnership between the provincial government, private sector organizations, nonprofits, and community leaders aimed at improving children's lives. Note that Alberta's Promise is not a fundraising initiative per se; it seeks to encourage and facilitate its partners to commit time and resources, including money, to the aims of the initiative.

This type of information is aimed primarily at increasing the number of people involved in philanthropy as well as the resources.

Channels and expected impact

The second category of information is targeted at philanthropists who would benefit from some guidance on certain aspects of philanthropy such as the intermediary channels that are currently available to them, the outcomes obtainable through those intermediaries, and the impact that those outcomes have had. This kind of information is behavior changing, and as such it affects the quality of philanthropy as opposed to the quantity of philanthropic flows.

Such information may be relevant to funders at the aggregate level, detailing total funds flowing to a specific sector compared to the needs in that sector, for example. It is also useful at the micro level, such as the amount of resources that are being contributed to a specific cause, compared to the overhead costs incurred by the intermediaries.

Providing philanthropists with accurate and detailed information about outcomes and impacts can have an important influence on the type of projects being funded. This can be useful for both governments and philanthropists in situations where philanthropists have indicated that they prefer to channel their donations to international causes because they believe that their contributions can have a larger impact on the lives of those in developing countries relative to those in industrialized ones.

Being able to access more information may lead to a reappraisal about the impact that different philanthropic activities can have. The result should be a more guided and focused philanthropy.

Priority sectors

The third category of information aims to provide philanthropists with information that will help them adopt a more strategic approach to their giving that dovetails with government policy. Governments can provide information about areas of development that are high-priority issues. This should help philanthropists engage in a dialogue with other philanthropic stakeholders in potential areas of mutual interest and collaboration, and should help direct philanthropic flows towards specific sectors.

Information about priority sectors is also directed at the quality and strategic impact of philanthropic flows more than the quantity. By highlighting the sectors that need more attention it leads to more focused philanthropic funding.

CO-FINANCING

Another way that governments can influence the philanthropic sector is through co-financing. By acting as philanthropists themselves, governments can affect the volume of philanthropic flows as well as their strategic impacts.

There are a number of different co-financing arrangements that governments can use. Direct funding can be used to tackle issues where private resources are simply insufficient to have the required impact. By forging partnerships with the private sector, it provides an opportunity for the government to strategically maximize the impact of the resources donated by the private sector by collaborating with it in areas that are of mutual interest.

In addition to direct funding, governments can enter into joint arrangements or partnerships with private sector philanthropists to advance mutually shared goals. The motives for partnering and specific arrangements may vary, and in turn can affect the amount of resources devoted to philanthropy and the channels used to allocate those resources. However, governments can use these types of partnerships as an opportunity to increase the strategic impact created by the private sector.

Governments will often partner with private entities in circumstances where the resources of either the private sector or the public sector acting alone are insufficient to address a particular challenge. These partnerships have other advantages for government beyond addressing developmental priorities. Such partnerships can provide governments with more flexibility to pursue and support activities that they might consider as having greater political risk, and that are potentially more contentious, by shifting the execution of these activities to their private partners.

By their very nature these types of public-private partnerships that are increasingly being advocated by governments, private entities, and international forums, are not part of a systematic program, but may only be formed at an opportune moment. At the same time it is also important to remember that the services or projects which governments are co-funding are not necessarily public services, or services that governments are expected to provide.

Some governments, however, have attempted to adopt a more systematic approach to co-financing partnerships through the establishment of government divisions tasked with facilitating public-private partnerships – usually in specific policy areas.

One country that has implemented this approach is the US, where the co-financing arrangements have been instituted by through divisions such as the Global Partnerships Initiative in the State Department and the Office of Social Innovation and Civic Participation within the White House.

Several international efforts have also assumed responsibility for facilitating such partnerships. Forums such as the World Economic Forum and the Clinton Global Initiative were created with the purpose of convening leaders from the public and private sectors (including philanthropic ones) with world leaders in order to facilitate partnerships to tackle some of the world's greatest challenges.

To encourage individuals or organizations to come forward with ideas about how to empower groups in need of financial support to implement their development ideas, some governments have established innovation funds and challenges. The US established a variety of innovation funds, such as the Corporation for National Security Social Innovation Fund, for example, in many different fields of interests including education, civil participation, and community engagement.

Innovation funds can also be targeted towards international challenges in the developing world such as the Group 20 (G20) Small- and Medium-Size Enterprise Financing Challenge that is looking for new ideas that will help facilitate the financing of small- and medium-sized businesses in the developing world.[128] Innovation funds provide the chance for people with innovative ideas to shine and the best ideas then receive funding to encourage these entrepreneurs to join the sector.

Some of the most prominent types of government financing that involve partnering with the private sector include matching funds programs, social impact bonds, religious funds programs, or participation in advanced market commitments, to target projects with strategic impacts. The level of private sector contribution varies from minimal with matching funds, for example, to fairly significant with advanced market commitments. Although these types of government partnerships mostly impact the quality or strategic impact of philanthropic flows, they nevertheless, indirectly also impact the level of philanthropic flows.

Matching funds programs are where the government matches contributions to specific causes that they identify as important. In Canada, for example, the government announced that it would match donations made to charitable organizations supporting the government's efforts in the Horn of Africa.

One example of matching funds is the UK Aid Match scheme. The UK government's objective is to create a scheme that allows the public some say on how the international development budget is disbursed. The Aid Match scheme is targeted at UK-based not-for-profit organizations that are working to reduce poverty in developing countries and planning to run a public appeal to raise at least £100,000.

Such an organization can apply to be a part of the scheme. In order to succeed it will need to demonstrate that it can deliver poverty reduction projects that achieve development results and are good value for money. The communications that form part of the appeal must also provide 'at least 400,000 opportunities to view.' Organizations will be selected on the basis of a number of criteria including their track record managing development activities; their commitment and ability to be transparent; clarity over objectives and consistency with DFID's objectives and values; and whether the proposed activities represent value for money.

For its part, the UK government has made available up to £120 million in grants over three years from 2013 to 2016, with two funding rounds per year. In addition at least £1 million per funding round is reserved for appeals run by small organizations – those with an annual income of less than £1 million averaged out over three years.[129]

A government might choose to resource-share with the private sector. Here the government combines its resources with the private sector and the resources pool is used by one of the parties involved, or by a third party, to implement the program. In 2007 the US government started the US-Palestinian Partnership, an effort by the US government that aimed to expand economic and educational opportunities for Palestinians. It pools resources from the US government with resources from private sector companies like Intel, Cisco, Google, and Microsoft.

Another route for government finances are religious funds programs. Here the government can channel funding through faith-based organizations, and may also be able to define the scope of what can be supported by philanthropy in these initiatives. In Abu Dhabi, for example, the Zakat Fund is a state-run organization (zakat is a form of obligatory alms giving, and one of the pillars of Islam). It collects funding from the federal government and numerous channels, including bank deposits, via its website and mobile technologies that facilitate zakat, and delivers the zakat to beneficiaries, such as individuals, families, and charities, as per Islamic criteria.

Advance market commitments (AMCs) are binding contracts used to guarantee a viable market if a certain product, such as a vaccine, is successfully developed. It is an innovative way to incentivize companies in creating and manufacturing vaccines primarily needed in low-income countries. This enables relevant companies, such as pharmaceutical companies, for example, to invest in the development of new products. A good example is the commitment by Canada, Italy, Norway, Russia, UK, and the Bill & Melinda Gates Foundation to put $1.5 billion into the launch of an AMC to develop a pneumonia and meningitis vaccine that would save seven million children by 2030.

AMC tackles a longstanding development problem – persistent market failures to develop and produce vaccines needed in poor countries due to perceptions of insufficient demand or market uncertainty. Donor countries commit money to subsidize the price of vaccines required by developing countries. The approach offers the necessary financial incentives by way of donor commitments for suppliers to develop the vaccines, including research and training staffs. By forging long-term contracts with suppliers, the program ensures lasting supply of vaccines for countries that need them.

A pilot AMC for pneumococcal vaccines was designed and launched on June 12, 2009 to demonstrate the feasibility of the program in creating affordable vaccines to meet growing demands. It also offers donor countries a mechanism for assessing the effectiveness of the program and expanding it to include other diseases. The program is designed to meet the vaccination demands of developing countries at a highly subsidized cost. The current price for the vaccine in industrialized countries is in the region of $70 per dose but, with the implementation of the program, the long-term price for developing countries will be $3.50. Initial estimates indicate that the program will be effective in preventing seven million childhood deaths due to pneumococcal disease by 2030.

The World Bank's role in the AMC Pneumo Initiative is to provide fiduciary support as well as legal and accounting systems, plus reporting functions as well as balance sheet support. CFPMI is overseeing the services for the AMC across the Bank.

Also, as we have seen in the Philanthropy 2.0 chapter (page 151), social impact bonds, a novel approach to tying investment opportunities and potential rewards to social outcomes, and structured financing where an initial layer of financing is underwritten to encourage further investment, provide co-financing opportunities for government.

The importance of impact evaluation

In order to make optimal programming and funding decisions it is essential to measure the impact of philanthropic activities. Official funders and a limited number of major philanthropic organizations understand the importance of metrics and measurement in philanthropy and this is reflected in the increasing support for international impact evaluation initiatives, such as the International Initiative on Impact Evaluation (3IE).

3IE was launched by both public and private entities in 2008. It was established in part to facilitate what are otherwise costly and difficult evaluations on what works in development programs and why. In this way it facilitates the increased use of impact evaluations by philanthropic organizations that are looking to increase the impact of their work and their ability to communicate impact to potential funders.

CAPACITY BUILDING

For the philanthropic sector to thrive, it requires appropriate physical and human capabilities. One common reason that philanthropic projects struggle is a lack of professional advice, experience, and training capacity, or the technological infrastructure required for information management. Take the experiences of bilateral aid agencies such as Spain's International Development Agency, which suggest that diaspora projects often suffer from the underuse of professional advice. [130]

Given their role as ODA providers, governments often have the underlying know-how and infrastructure that can be deployed to help efficiently manage philanthropic flows. However, enabling this transfer can be a challenge, given that many of the aid agencies rely on external consultants.

Setting priorities, identifying potential areas of mutual interest and collaboration, and providing professional advice on financial management and strategic giving, are just some of the areas where governments are able to help to provide guidance to philanthropists. The government can either leverage its know-how as an ODA provider, acting as the professional advisor, or alternatively it might seek professional and experienced partners to provide expert advice.

The development of a well-informed and experienced work force is very important in the philanthropic sector. Most organizations try to maintain low administrative overheads in order to maximize the funding directed towards philanthropic activities, and this can have a negative impact on the training of employees and volunteers. Public awareness programs and special training and workshops provided in collaboration with the leading organizations can help build much needed human capacity.

It is often the private sector that adopts the training and support role. Take the Ford Foundation's involvement in Vietnam, where it helped Vietnamese-American activist Dao Spencer to bring back Vietnamese-Americans to Vietnam via the American NGO PACT. The idea was for the Vietnamese-Americans to offer their expertise in areas such as education and health, supported by the Ford Foundation.[131]

Training and capacity building in diaspora organizations can also benefit from donor support. One effective way of providing this support is through umbrella organizations such as the federations of Mexico and other hometown associations (HTAs), or the African Foundation for Development (AFFORD) in the United Kingdom. Identifying the specific needs of diaspora groups and the specific challenges of working in their country of origin are critical to making such training initiatives productive. The gathering and dissemination of relevant information from these countries can provide insights into the challenges of undertaking development projects in specific countries.[132] An organization such as the US federal aid agency USAID is well placed to provide this information via its missions in the countries of origin for a particular diaspora, for example.

Operating model

The governance structure of the philanthropy sector, or the operating model, consists of all the entities, public and private, that are involved in operating and regulating the sector. Given the lack of data, it is hard to measure the level of development of the philanthropy sector. But one way of assessing its maturity is to look at the number of NGOs (per 100,000 of the population) and the extent to which the civil society is established in a country – a relatively good indicator of the number of philanthropic organizations, in the absence of more reliable data.

In addition to using the development of civil society in a country as a metric, the absolute level and volume of philanthropy is almost always higher the more developed a country is, providing another indicator to use in assessing the maturity of the sector. In more developed countries, the philanthropic sector is also likely to be a lot more regulated and more formal, with more channels available that are transparent in their functions.

Depending on the types of regulations that governments enact, different divisions of government may be responsible for enacting policies that affect philanthropy. In some cases, several government divisions are responsible for policies affecting the sector, while in others governments have established entities or tasked divisions of government with mandates exclusively focused on philanthropy.

Some of these entities assume several roles with respect to the sector – regulation and partnership, for example. The nature of these entities also differs based on the main sources of the philanthropic flows that they are targeting. For instance, entities in developing countries, those typically characterized by a less developed philanthropic sector, that are tasked with attracting philanthropic resources from outside the country, differ from those in industrialized countries that are principally oriented towards philanthropy that originates domestically.

Another distinction worth making between countries of different development levels is the third sector participation. Although countries with less developed governments have less developed philanthropic sectors, they are generally characterized by a relatively lower number of NGOs. (This might not apply to all countries. For instance, in the case of India and numerous LAC countries, the country could have a less developed philanthropic sector but a high number of informal NGOs and community-based organizations.) In such countries, the third sector plays a more substantial role because governments are typically weak and financially constrained.

As previously mentioned, although the operating model is contingent upon the development level of the country's philanthropic sector, some characteristics are common everywhere. Globally, philanthropy-regulating government entities are not involved in financing philanthropic programs. Nevertheless, they usually direct their philanthropic flows either directly into philanthropic partnerships with the private sector, or channel it through funding of non-governmental philanthropic organizations.

Countries that have a developed philanthropic sector tend to perform the three other roles – regulation, information, and capacity-building – through one centralized entity. Countries that have developing philanthropic sectors, on the other hand, tend to have separate regulatory entities. In rare cases, like Pakistan, the government delegates some of its regulatory roles, such as certification of organizations, for example, to local NGOs.

The power of the many

While high-net-worth individuals made a considerable impact through their generous philanthropy, the potential impact that the many different types of philanthropy could make collectively is huge. When the comparative advantages of philanthropy are effectively harnessed, it is a potent force capable of improving societal welfare at a significant scale.

Private philanthropic engagement is often driven by the characteristics of individual philanthropists, many of which are not directly affected by governments. Nevertheless, government policy and engagement have the potential to influence certain characteristics, the channels used by philanthropists, the types of outcomes their engagement supports, and more importantly the transparency of these flows of funding.

This is the case in many countries, where an abundance of resources and a capacity for creativity and ambition could be harnessed to increase the strategic impact of the philanthropic sector. In order to do so, these countries will need to do a number of things. They must establish coherent objectives and identify the obstacles to achieving those objectives. They must have frameworks, structures, and interventions that accurately address any obstacles identified and that serve to enhance the efficacy and transparency of the philanthropic sector.

The landscape of the philanthropy sector and the ways in which governments can set about influencing it are outlined in this chapter. The opportunity is there. Now governments need to take the necessary steps to seize that opportunity.

15
A philanthropy roadmap

Philanthropy has traditionally been viewed as a type of funding that is predominately private and motivated by altruism. However, there are signs of a shift in the world of philanthropy towards a form of philanthropy that is more strategic, with more focus on outcome performance. Taken together with other changes such as technological advances, innovative financing methods, and a generation of philanthropists with an entrepreneurial mindset, it creates an environment amenable to using these transfers to achieve greater developmental impact.

Governments can play a key role in increasing the impact that philanthropic flows of money have. To do so requires a strategy to guide government's engagement within the philanthropic sector; a framework that shapes a set of interventions, passive and active, designed to get more from philanthropy.

GOVERNMENT OBJECTIVES

A well-designed strategy is one where outcomes are capable of being monitored and measured. This means identifying and defining objectives at the outset. What are the reasons for engaging in the philanthropic sector? What does government hope to achieve? It might be, for example, that the government's objective is to increase philanthropic flows, to enable higher impact contributions, to influence the allocation of philanthropy, or something else altogether.

In many countries the role of the private sector is well established in terms of its involvement provision of public services. There is also, however, scope for third sector organizations, including philanthropists and associated intermediaries, to assist with providing public services. Engaging philanthropists and their intermediaries in this way could be another objective.

Furthermore, when philanthropy is targeted towards initiatives outside the source country, this could be viewed as meeting international challenges. As such it could in turn be construed as an extension of a government's aid policy. Thus another objective might be to try and couple foreign aid efforts with major philanthropic flows, as a complimentary source of funding.

Determining the government's objectives at the outset helps guide all the other decisions required to establish a strategic framework to guide any intervention connected to philanthropic giving.

SCOPE AND ROLE

Based on its objectives, the government will decide on the role it wishes to adopt and the actions it will get involved in. At the same time it will consider the scope of its role depending on factors such as the resources at its disposal. Some aspects of the objectives might be better delivered by other organizations, or in partnership with other organizations.

In the context of increasing the impact of philanthropy, governments can act as information providers, regulators, capacity builders, even co-financers. For example, there may be a lack of creativity and innovation in the sector. A government may decide that it is best placed to encourage innovation and creativity by setting an example and acting as a philanthropist.

However, a government may believe that the market is better placed to create the conditions in which creativity and innovation can flourish, free of government intervention. A third option would be to create an environment of creativity and innovation in the philanthropy arena by partnering with private entities.

The scope of a government's role may also be influenced by whether the type of philanthropy that the government wants to influence originates domestically or internationally, or is due to be targeted at domestic or international outcomes.

Having decided the type and scope of its role, a government will decide on the specific action it wishes to take, whether that is in the form of legislation, regulation, or policy. For example, what aspects (if any) of the philanthropic sector could be improved through changes in the legal and policy framework – the operation of philanthropic organizations, the establishment of philanthropic organizations, or contributions to philanthropic organizations.

The government may create new tax laws to encourage philanthropic giving, for example, or attempt to influence people's actions through behavioral science-related techniques. As well as introducing new legislation, regulations or policies, deregulation, the repeal of laws, and changes in policy direction are also possible.

INSTITUTIONAL SET-UP AND ORGANIZATIONAL ARRANGEMENTS

Based on the constraints the government is aiming to address, the government must decide what type of infrastructure is needed to achieve these ends. Would the roles that the government wants to play be best achieved through the creation of a new government entity, the establishment of a philanthropy office within an existing government entity, the creation of new programs, or the introduction of new policies? If the requisite infrastructure does not exist the government should decide what actions are needed to create it.

Conclusion – the transformation agenda

This book demonstrates the huge potential for improving the lives of people across the globe. The three financial forces – aid, remittances and philanthropy – represent a significant proportion of the wealth that is directed towards improving social and economic conditions in developing economies. Together they represent over a trillion dollars annually. And these financial flows, compared in Figure 4, continue to grow.

For many developing countries the money received from three forms of income transfer easily outweigh other funds available for improving social, environmental, and economic conditions. As highlighted previously, for example, in Lebanon remittances represented 45 percent of annual financial inflows, significantly greater than the 25 percent contribution from annual foreign direct investment.

These sources of funding have a number of advantages. For a start they are more reliable and less volatile than other forms of funding, such as foreign direct investment, equities, or debt which are linked to investment and investment returns, and are therefore likely to be more sensitive to movements in financial markets and to global economic metrics. This was evident from events following the 2008 financial crisis. The crisis caused turmoil in equity and debt markets and had a significant impact on foreign currencies and global interest rates. Aid, remittances, and philanthropy, which are countercyclical and flow in bad times as well as good, remained relatively resilient, however. When governments and investors

182 THE GIVING WORLD

Figure 4: Givin-omics – the three forces compared

	ODA *Flows of official financing comprising contributions of donor government agencies, to developing countries.*	Philanthropy *A welfare-enhancing donation of a share of an individual or organization's sources.*	Remittances *Transfers of money by migrant workers to their home country.*
Source of income transfer	Public *The source of official development assistance is always the government.*	Public and / or Private *The source of philanthropy can be the government, individuals and/or corporations.*	Private *The source of remittances is migrant individuals.*
Beneficiaries	Public *Aid recipients are typically international governments, multilaterals and/or bilateral organizations.*	Public and / or private *Philanthropic beneficiaries can be private or public in nature and either local or international.*	Private *Recipients of remittances are typically the family members and/or the community of the immigrant workers.*
Giving target level	MODERATELY TARGETED ODA beneficiaries are governments as a whole, and or government programs.	LEAST TARGETED Philanthropy beneficiaries at most times are entirely unknown	HIGHLY TARGETED Remittance beneficiaries are highly targeted where their individual identities are known
"Cause"	ODA is at times sent for a specific cause, and at others times is not	Philanthropy can be sent for certain specific causes, but can also be transferred out of religious or moral obligation.	Remittances are always sent for a specific cause.
Motivations	Geopolitical Developmental Charity Humanitarian	Altruistic Developmental Charity Identity-associated	To support family members and/or the community Developmental

get nervous about leveraging in developing economies, they will quickly move their investment focus and funds elsewhere. Yet aid, remittances, and philanthropy money often remains.

Indeed, although emerging markets may be out of favor, elsewhere developed economies may be thriving. As a result, governments are happy to continue maintaining and even increasing aid budgets. With a growing economy, migrants are able to obtain work, benefit from wage rises, and send more money home. Individuals, organizations, and trusts have discretionary income that can be directed at philanthropic giving.

The same applies if one region in the world is in difficulty. If growth stalls in Asia, then aid, remittances, and philanthropy from those countries affected may dip temporarily too. But the aid, remittances, and philanthropy received from the rest of the world should continue to flow.

While these transfers of income already contribute to improving people's lives, they could have much more of an impact than they do at present. There are a number of reasons that these sources of income are not being used to maximum effect. One reason, in the case of remittances and philanthropy, is the original source of the funding. In the case of philanthropy and remittances a lot of the giving is from private individuals, and much of it is made on an ad hoc basis. This means it is difficult to coordinate funds towards larger projects. For example, the majority of remittances are relatively small amounts made by individual migrants and sent back to their families to fund day-to-day living costs. Furthermore, they may be intermittent, varying depending on the employment and pay fortunes of the migrants.

Equally, a lot of giving has been primarily altruistic. As such, there has been less examination of, or accountability for, its efficient use. In the case of philanthropy, for example, the focus has traditionally been on the giving element: how to raise more funds and where to direct those funds. With remittances, migrants worry about little more than whether they have funds to send home and that those funds reach the intended recipient. Even with ODA much of the emphasis has been on amount – the provision of a specified percentage of GDP, for example.

However, important new trends are emerging in these three forms of giving. There are signs of a more collective approach to remittances, for example. Remittances are being pooled through the medium of home associations, and a number of more sophisticated innovative investment approaches. There is also a trend towards giving which is not solely altruistic. Donor countries such as China, for instance, are tying aid to the objectives of the donor. And a new generation of philanthropists are seeking impact through their philanthropy, and practicing new types of philanthropy such as venture philanthropy and entrepreneurial philanthropy.

These new approaches encourage greater care over the fate of donated funds. As a result, there is greater governance and accountability, with donors focusing on outcomes and objectives. In many instances it is no longer enough just to give. In addition to giving it is necessary to ensure that any money given is used efficiently and that certain objectives are met.

This is where governments can play a key role. Governments already have an impact on these three flows but there is much more that they can do to promote the strategic use of aid, remittances, and philanthropy. Furthermore, it is not only through regulation that governments can act. In addition, they can take a proactive stance by introducing policies that encourage the effective use of the three flows. They can do this even where the source of that money is private.

And there are many synergies between these three forces. For example, matching remittances through aid money is likely to increase the impact of both flows by increasing the scale of any intervention and allowing for more targeted applications. Similarly with philanthropy, aid donors can work with large foundations to address global challenges such as disease eradication and climate change.

With philanthropy and remittances there are potential synergies available via the diaspora, who may assume the roles of philanthropists and remitter at the same time. Rather than sending remittances to their families they can, for example, channel their money to larger development-focused causes.

There are many more instances of these kinds of synergies, so although it is important to tackle each flow, it is equally important to seek out the synergies between them.

To do any of this, to maximize the individual flows and leverage the synergies between them, governments need to develop an overarching strategic framework that governs their approach to dealing with aid, remittances, and philanthropy. The framework should cover the points detailed in the book and summarized at the end of each section.

There are four essential elements of such a strategic framework: what the government's objectives are; its role; the role of stakeholders; and judging success, metrics, and monitoring.

WHAT ARE THE GOVERNMENT'S OBJECTIVES?

Governments must decide on their overall objectives with regards to the three flows. For example, what mix of development, humanitarian, and geopolitical aid objectives are preferred? Will aid be assistance or investment driven? Will it be explicitly tied? To what extent does government want to intervene in the transfer of remittances out of the country by immigrant workers, or indeed the transfer of remittances into the country by its diaspora? It might only wish to facilitate the transfer and receipt of remittances, or it may want to go a step further and influence the amount of money sent and received and the uses of that money. Similarly, governments should decide how much influence they wish to exert over philanthropic funding, from enabling greater sums to be raised to shaping the direction and objectives of donations.

THE ROLE OF GOVERNMENT

In order to meet their objectives, governments must decide what kinds of actions are most likely to deliver those objectives, and who should take and be accountable for those actions. A common decision, for example, concerns whether a legislative and regulatory approach is appropriate or if a policy would be more effective, or a mix of the two. With philanthropy, for example, a regulatory approach might encompass registration and licensing of philanthropic organizations, and the impact of taxation; for remittances, policies designed to provide information and promote awareness, and encourage the use of legitimate mechanism may be useful.

Another key choice is whether to pursue passive or active policies. Does the government want to use more sophisticated financial products, for example? This might include diaspora bonds or the securitization of remittances in order to enable the use of those remittances for large developmental projects, or social impact bonds in order to link philanthropic giving and social objectives, tied to performance metrics. Does it want to facilitate some kind of matched funds initiative, whether connected with remittance pooling and migrant associations, or a particular philanthropic endeavor?

As we have seen, government intervention can range from the lightest behavioral nudge to the heaviest sanction-backed law.

The means through which governments act must also be determined. For government's part it may act directly through existing departments, set up a dedicated department, or task a government agency. For example, when setting up an aid management system, governments can decide to centralize aid through a standalone department; part centralize where responsibilities are split between a government department and separate agency; split aid responsibilities up depending on their purpose; or even assign it to departments responsible for different global regions, if such departments exist. With philanthropy, governments might want to establish a philanthropy office within an existing government entity. For remittances, governments might work through a range of government bodies, whether that is a finance ministry, local government institutions such as federal banks, or overseas offices in recipient countries.

THE ROLE OF STAKEHOLDERS

What role will other stakeholders play – what cooperation and collaboration is possible? There are limits to what governments can achieve alone;

so that aid, remittances, and philanthropy can have the most impact, governments should be keen to engage with a variety of stakeholders. Collaboration and cooperation with other stakeholders is one of the most important aspects of building a successful strategy to maximize the impact of aid, remittances, and philanthropy.

As well as governments in other countries, there are very many organizations and institutions, both in the donor and recipient countries, that can help. These include NGOs, international agencies, multilateral organizations, central banks, commercial banks and other financial service providers, home associations, social entrepreneurs and their associated ventures, and numerous corporations from engineering firms to telecoms providers, pharmaceutical giants to internet technology start-ups. This is particularly true, for example, if a government wants to harness the power of modern technology as part of its strategy, as technological innovation and expertise often resides outside of government. Take philanthropy where social media and internet-based crowdfunding platforms are revolutionizing philanthropic giving on a global scale. Mobile phone technology and smart payment systems are doing the same with remittances.

WHAT DOES SUCCESS LOOK LIKE? METRICS AND MONITORING

If governments are going to make the effort to develop a strategy that enables more productive use of aid, remittances, and philanthropy, it makes sense for them to check how successful those efforts have been. This will depend on their initial objectives, and how those objectives were defined. Assuming that strategic objectives have been mapped out and clearly stated, it is possible to identify drivers that contribute to those objectives. The performance relating to both the drivers and the outcomes they lead to can be monitored and measured using new or existing metrics.

In philanthropy it may be a case of encouraging new forms of philanthropy such as venture philanthropy, for example, enabling initiatives like social impact bonds, and supporting steps to standardize impact measurement such as the International Initiative on Impact Evaluation. With aid, donor countries may introduce a single reporting framework, implemented across all the donor entities. Alternatively other bodies delivering the aid may use their own performance management systems but be required to report back on common metrics. With remittances, much of the challenge is encouraging formal, regulated means of transferring money, as this allows better data collection and performance monitoring and assessment. Through collaboration with the governments of the countries receiving remittances, as well as with other organizations, it is possible to measure the performance of remittance-funded outcomes. This is especially the case where government strategy is directed at initiatives such as pooled remittances, for example.

The introduction to this book highlights the many challenges that the world faces, from climate change to the pressures of population growth, poverty and hunger to poor health, resource shortages to humanitarian crises. Trillions of dollars have been spent trying to alleviate these problems. Yet while some progress has been made, there is still a long way to go. The ecosystem of stakeholders involved in meeting these challenges is beginning to understand, if it does not already, that while new sources of funding are invaluable, it is not just the amount spent that matters, but how it is spent, and what is achieved as a result.

This book shows how the three financial forces are being used to improve people's lives, primarily in developing countries. But it also demonstrates the potential to substantially increase the impact of these funds. Most importantly, though, it reveals how governments can play a central role in leveraging their impact, and in many cases already are.

I am optimistic about the future, optimistic about the power of people to change the world for the better. Governments are not faceless institutions; more often than not they are filled with passionate public servants, committed to creating a better society. The aim of this book is not to tell governments what to do or how to do it. Instead its aim is to highlight what is possible. For anyone interested in, or involved with, tackling many of the difficult challenges facing mankind, I hope that this book, the insights and examples, the roadmaps that it contains, can help them transform the giving world.

Glossary

A glossary of remittance terms may be useful.

Active (remittance) policies: The tactics some governments use to directly influence remitters' activities, including the projects the remitters' support or the investments they make.

Balance of payments: A tally of the monetary transactions a country has with the rest of the world. Remittances can offset deficits in the balance of payments, lowering the recipient country's credit risk.

Collective remittance: Remittances pooled by migrants from a specific country or region. Collective remittances usually target a specific purpose.

Donor (or sender) country: The country from which the remittance money is sent.

Formal transfer systems: When migrants use banks, post offices, or money transfer organizations to remit funds.

Hawala services: The network of informal money changers that many remitters rely on to transfer money cheaply and reliably.

Individual remittance: Remittances sent by a single person, often to family members back home.

Informal transfer systems: When remitters carry money home themselves or send it via a friend, relative or Hawaladar (money changer).

Passive (remittance) policies: Mechanisms that governments use to indirectly influence remitters' activities, including directing them toward lower-fee remittance services and informing them of investment opportunities in their countries of origin.

Recipient country: The country to which remittances are sent.

Remittance: Money that a migrant sends back to his country of origin, either to assist relatives, invest or support a development project.

South-North migration: The movement of migrants north, to countries of greater wealth and economic opportunity.

South-South migration: The movement of migrants from one developing nation to another, usually for perceived economic benefit. Less frequently, the migration is prompted by political conflict or violence in the homeland.

About the author

Mona Hammami Hijazi is a director at the Office of Strategic Affairs, Abu Dhabi Crown Prince Court. Her role includes analysis of social and economic developments globally and locally, and drafting publications and white papers to influence policy making.

Prior to joining the Crown Prince Court, she was a lead associate at Booz and Company, focusing on a wide range of macroeconomic and public policy issues including large-scale transformation, social and labor policies, agriculture policy reform, and structuring PPP projects. She also worked as an economist with the International Monetary Fund (IMF) and the UN Economic and Social Commission for Western Asia (ESCWA). She has authored several articles and policy papers including 'Determinants of Public Private Partnerships', published by the IMF. Her publications also include the book *Looking Ahead: The 50 Trends that Matter*.

Hammami Hijazi holds a PhD in Development Studies from the University of Oxford and a Master in Public Administration International Development from Harvard Kennedy school. She is a recipient of both the H.R.H. Princess Banderi Al-Faisal Public Service Fellowship and Sheikh Abdulaziz Al-Tuwaijri International Public Service Fellowship. In 2010, she set up her own Graduate Fellowship fund at the Harvard Kennedy School. She serves on the board for the Harvard Arab Alumni association and Path Arabia and is the founding curator of the World Economic Forum Abu Dhabi Global Shapers Hub and a member of the Welfare Association.

Acknowledgments

Completing this piece of work would have not been possible without the assistance of many people, indeed, without a journey full of teachers and colleagues who have shaped the field of development and my own views of it. In particular, I hugely appreciate the support of Dr. Robin Niblett, director of Chatham House, for his contribution and insights into the book.

I am immensely thankful to my colleagues Rabih Abouchakra, Michel Khoury, and Fiona Paua Schwab for their comments, guidance and mentoring throughout the book development process. Without their input, the road we had to travel to complete this book would have been much rockier. For their contributions and research, I would like to thank Ayah Mahjoub, Roula Rbeiz, Alanoud Madhi, Rasha Al Attar Solh, and Jad Mneymneh.

I would like to also thank Stuart Crainer and Des Dearlove, the founders of Thinkers50, for their input, support, and enthusiasm. Their colleague Steve Coomber was a vital member of the team in helping shape and transform my ideas and research into a book.

Finally, I would like to thank my husband Rabih Hijazi for being my beacon of balance in trying times. Thank you for your endless support, valid comments, continuous guidance and encouragement, and for always believing in me. I would also love to thank my family for being there whenever I needed them. Thank you for keeping up with me and getting me past my many moments of doubt.

Notes

1. All amounts are American dollars unless otherwise stated.
2. *Credit Suisse Global Wealth Report 2015.* www.credit-suisse.com/articles/news-and-expertise/2015/10/en/global-wealth-in-2015-underlying-trends-remain-positive.html
3. www.worldbank.org/en/topic/poverty/overview
4. *The State of Food Insecurity in the World,* May 2015. Food & Agriculture Organization of the United Nations. www.fao.org/3/a-i4646e.pdf
5. www.who.int/mediacentre/factsheets/fs395/en/
6. www.who.int/mediacentre/factsheets/fs094/en/
7. www.who.int/mediacentre/factsheets/fs348/en/
8. *Progress on Sanitation and Drinking Water - 2015 update and MDG assessment,* UNICEF and World Health Organization, 2015; www.wssinfo.org/fileadmin/user_upload/resources/JMP-Update-report-2015_English.pdf
9. Ibid.
10. Ibid.
11. *IPCC AR5 Synthesis Report,* Presentation of the IPCC Fifth Assessment Report - United Nations, Nairobi, 23 February. The Intergovernmental Panel on Climate Change, 2015; www.ipcc.ch/pdf/presentations/Kenya%20Tanzania%20outreach%20event.pdf
12. http://apps.who.int/ebola/current-situation/ebola-situation-report-28-october-2015
13. http://data.unhcr.org/syrianrefugees/regional.php
14. http://drrportal.gov.np/; Nepal Earthquake – Fact Sheet #21, Fiscal Year (Fy) 2015, June 25, 2015. USAid.

www.usaid.gov/sites/default/files/documents/1866/nepal_eq_fs21_06-25-2015.pdf
15   http://esa.un.org/unpd/wpp/DVD/Files/2_Indicators%20(Probabilistic%20Projections)/UN_PPP2015_Output_PopTot.xls
16   *World Population Prospects: The 2015 Revision, Key Findings and Advance Tables, Working Paper No. ESA/P/WP.241,* United Nations, New York, 2015.
17   *World Urbanization Prospects: The 2014 Revision.* United Nations, Department of Economic and Social Affairs, Population Division (2014); http://esa.un.org/unpd/wup/
18   *Speed and the City: Can Humans Keep Up?* By Mona Hammami Hijazi.
19   *The Millennium Development Goals Report, 2015.* United Nations, New York. 2015.www.un.org/millenniumgoals/2015_MDG_Report/pdf/MDG%202015%20PR%20Key%20Facts%20Global.pdf
20   Ibid.
21   Ibid.
22   Ibid.
23   *Goals for Development: History, Prospects, and Costs* by Devarajan, Shantayanan, Miller, Margaret J., Swanson, Eric V World Bank, Washington, D.C, 2002.; www.worldbank.org/html/extdr/mdgassessment.pdf
24   Shame on me: Why it was wrong to cost the Millennium Development Goals, Shanta Devarajan, Future Development, Brookings.edu, March 2, 2015; www.brookings.edu/blogs/future-development/posts/2015/03/02-costing-millennium-development-goals-devarajan
25   It's Up To The World: Pay For The Global Goals Or Buy Everyone A Latte by Malaka Gharib, NPR.org, September 29, 2015; www.npr.org/sections/goatsandsoda/2015/09/29/444437131/who-s-footing-the-bill-how-to-pay-for-the-u-n-s-3-trillion-plan-to-end-poverty
26   www.un.org/development/desa/en/news/financing/final-push-for-ffd3.html
27   *Report of the Intergovernmental Committee of Experts on Sustainable Development Financing,* United Nations, New York, 2014; www.un.org/esa/ffd/wp-content/uploads/2014/12/ICESDF.pdf
28   *Migration and Development Brief 22*, World Bank, April 11, 2014; https://siteresources.worldbank.org/INTPROSPECTS/Resources/334934-1288990760745/MigrationandDevelopmentBrief22.pdf;

World Bank, *Migration and Remittances Factbook 2011*, 2010; http://siteresources.worldbank.org/INTLAC/Resources/Factbook2011-Ebook.pdf

29 *Index of Global Philanthropy and Remittances 2013,* Hudson Institute, 2013, Washington, D.C.; http://www.hudson.org/research/9914-2013-index-of-global-philanthropy-and-remittances-with-a-special-report-on-emerging-economies

30 *30 Case Studies in Global Health: Millions Saved* by Ruth Levine, Jones & Bartlett, 2007, page 50.

31 www.cdc.gov/parasites/onchocerciasis/gen_info/faqs.html

32 Project profile: African Program for Onchocerciasis Control - Phase III, Foreign Affairs, Trade and Development Canada, Government of Canada; www.acdi-cida.gc.ca/cidaweb/cpo.nsf/vWebMCSAZEn/C9B2C8494C4CE5F98525757800371F12

33 'Nigeria: Donors allot $31m to eliminate river blindness', Muda Oyeniran. *Nigerian Tribune*; http://africanbrains.net/2011/01/20/nigeria-donors-allot-31m-to-eliminate-river-blindness

34 *Food Aid and the Developing World: Four African Case Studies,* by Christopher Stevens. Croom Helm, Jan 1, 1979; *Continuing the commitment: agricultural development in the Sahel.* Congress of the U.S., Office of Technology Assessment, Washington, D.C., 1986.

35 *Analyzing Growth in Burkina Faso over the Last Four Decades* by Savadogo, Kimseyinga, Siaka Coulibaly, and Coleen A. McCracken. African Economic Research Consortium Growth Project, 2003. http://dspace.africaportal.org/jspui/bitstream/123456789/32041/1/BurkinaFaso.pdf?1

36 *The Green Revolution* pp1-13, Fitzgerald-Moore, P., and B.J. Parai, Ucalgary.ca. University of Calgary, 1996: www.ucalgary.ca/~pfitzger/green.pdf; Case 20, The Green Revolution, Rockefeller Foundation, 1943, Scott Kohler; https://cspcs.sanford.duke.edu/sites/default/files/descriptive/green_revolution.pdf; *Green Revolution: Curse or Blessing.* International Food Policy Research Institute: Sustainable Options for Ending Hunger and Poverty. International Food Policy Research Institute. 2002. http://oregonstate.edu/instruct/bi430-fs430/Documents-2004/2B-GREEN%20REV/GreenRevo-Curse-or-Blessing-IFPRI.pdf

37 www.usaid.gov/results-data/success-stories/potable-wells-improve-water-access-chad
38 Ibid.
39 www.oecd.org/dac/stats/officialdevelopmentassistancedefinitionandcoverage.htm
40 Official development assistance: Aid 2.0, *Economist,* August 13, 2011; www.economist.com/node/21525899.
41 www.oecd.org/dac/stats/the07odagnitarget-ahistory.htm/ Original text from *DAC Journal* 2002, Vol 3 No 4, pages III-9 –III-11 Revised June 2010; www.oecd.org/dac/stats/45539274.pdf;www.oecd.org/dac/stats/documentupload/OnePercentTarget.pdf
42 www.oecd.org/dac/stats/development-aid-stable-in-2014-but-flows-to-poorest-countries-still-falling.htm
43 These figures could overestimate levels of giving due to the potential for double counting of disbursements and commitments. The data reporting is also not necessarily in line with the DAC methodology.
44 Aid with Chinese Characteristics: Chinese Foreign Aid and Development Finance meet the OECD-DAC Aid Regime, by Deborah Bräutigam, *Journal of International Development,* 2011; www.american.edu/sis/faculty/upload/Brautigam-Aid-with-Chinese-Characteristics.pdf
45 *Harmonising Donor Practices for Effective Aid Delivery, Good Practice Papers,* A DAC Reference Document, OECD, 2003.
46 Effective Aid Management: Twelve lessons from DAC peer reviews, OECD 2008.
47 As at November 2014.
48 As at November 2014.
49 In the language of international affairs, 'The North' typically refers to wealthy developed countries and 'The South' refers to poorer developing countries. ODA flows have traditionally been North to South.
50 www.oecd.org/dac/effectiveness/busanpartnership.htm
51 Aid still benefits companies from donor countries by Claire Provost, *Guardian,* September, 2011; www.theguardian.com/global-development/2011/sep/07/aid-benefits-donor-countries-companies
52 Ibid.

53 'Chinese Development Aid in Africa: What, Where, Why, and How Much? By Deborah Bräutigam, In *Rising China: Global Challenges and Opportunities,* Jane Golley and Ligang Song, eds, Canberra: Australia National University Press, 2011, pp. 203-223; www.american.edu/sis/faculty/upload/brautigam-chinese-aid-in-africa.pdf
54 India's foreign aid program catches up with its global ambitions by Lorenzo Piccio, Devex.com, May 2013; www.devex.com/news/india-s-foreign-aid-program-catches-up-with-its-global-ambitions-80919
55 http://siteresources.worldbank.org/INTPROSPECTS/Resources/334934-1288990760745/MigrationandDevelopmentBrief24.pdf; www.un.org/en/development/desa/population/migration/data/estimates2/estimatestotal.shtml
56 www.oecd.org/els/mig/38840502.pdf for more information
57 Ibid. – 55.
58 http://articles.economictimes.indiatimes.com/2015-01-30/news/58625677_1_2008-fdi-inflows-services-sector
59 Ibid. – 55.
60 Ibid. – 55.
61 http://esa.un.org/unmigration/documents/The_number_of_international_migrants.pdf
62 Ibid.
63 www.practicelink.com/magazine/vital-stats/physician-compensation-worldwide/
64 The World Bank's Remittance and Migration Data; World Bank Indicators.
65 http://siteresources.worldbank.org/INTPROSPECTS/Resources/334934-1288990760745/RemittanceData_Outflows_Apr2015.xls
66 Ibid. – 55.
67 http://siteresources.worldbank.org/INTPROSPECTS/Resources/334934-1288990760745/RemittanceData_Inflows_Apr2015.xls
68 Ibid. – 55.
69 Can International Remittances Be Unproductive in Recipient Countries? Not Really! By Zahid Hussain, End Poverty in South Asia blog, WorldBank.org, February, 2014; http://blogs.worldbank.org/

endpovertyinsouthasia/can-international-remittances-be-unproductive-recipient-countries-not-really
70 Remittances and growth, Gone missing, *Economist,* August, 2014; www.economist.com/blogs/freeexchange/2014/08/remittances-and-growth
71 Ibid.
72 Remittance Corridors: New Rivers of Gold, *Economist,* April 28–May 4, 2012; www.economist.com/node/21553458
73 Philippines still relies on remittances amid struggle for foreign investment by Kotaro Hidaka, *Nikkei Asian Review,* October 2015; http://asia.nikkei.com/Politics-Economy/Economy/Philippines-still-relies-on-remittances-amid-struggle-for-foreign-investment
74 High remittances helping Lebanon to weather financial crisis, Al Bawaba, August, 2015; www.albawaba.com/business/high-remittances-helping-lebanon-weather-financial-crisis-728252
75 Do Remittances Affect Poverty and Inequality? Evidence from Mali, F. Gubert, T. Lassourd and S. Mesple-Somps. Document De Travel DT/2010-08, Paris-Dauphine University.; http://siteresources.worldbank.org/INTTRADERESEARCH/Resources/544824-1323963330969/8322197-1323963839213/Gubert_Lassourd_Mesple-Somps.pdf; Remittances, poverty, inequality and welfare: Evidence from the Central Plateau of Burkina Faso, F Wouterse, *The Journal of Development Studies* 46 (4), 771-789; http://www.iadb.org/res/publications/pubfiles/pubWP-571.pdf; http://gdri.dreem.free.fr/wp-content/d53-ebekelegoff_final.pdf
76 Africans' remittances outweigh Western aid by Mark Doyle, BBC News, April 2013; www.bbc.com/news/world-africa-22169474
77 The Development of Home Town Associations in the United States and the Use of Social Remittances in Mexico,' in *Sending Money Home: Hispanic Remittances and Community Development,* ed. R. O. de la Garza and B. L. Lowell (Lanham, MD: Rowman & Littlefield Publishers, 2002); http://essays.ssrc.org/remittances_anthology/wp-content/uploads/2009/08/Topic_9_Alarcon.pdf
78 www.ifad.org/remittances/pub/money_europe.pdf
79 www.smart-transfer.com/customer_service.html
80 https://remittanceprices.worldbank.org/en/corridor
81 *Unauthorized immigrant population stable for half a decade* by Jeffrey S.

Passel and D'Vera Cohn, Pew Research Center, July 22, 2015; www.pewresearch.org/fact-tank/2015/07/22/unauthorized-immigrant-population-stable-for-half-a-decade/;
Illegal immigration to Europe shows sharp rise by David Barrett, *Telegraph,* May 2014.; www.telegraph.co.uk/news/uknews/immigration/10865652/Illegal-immigration-to-Europe-shows-sharp-rise.html

82 *Remittances: An Underutilized Policy Tool,* August 2010, Crown Prince Court, Emirate of Abu Dhabi.

83 www.coha.org/money-money-money-remittances-and-microbanking-in-haiti/#_ftn6

84 Haiti Remittances Key to Earthquake Recovery, World Bank.org, May 2010; http://web.worldbank.org/WBSITE/EXTERNAL/NEWS/0,,contentMDK:22582923~pagePK:64257043~piPK:437376~theSitePK:4607,00.html

85 Maximizing the development impact of Remittances, Trade and Development Board, Trade and Development Commission, Expert Meeting on Maximizing the Development Impact of Remittances, UNCTAD, Geneva, 14–15 February 2011; http://unctad.org/en/docs/ciem4d2_en.pdf

86 Ibid. box 3. P12.

87 Ibid.

88 *Report to the Congress on the Use of the ACH System and Other Payment Mechanisms for Remittance Transfers to Foreign Countries,* April 2013. Board of Governors of the Federal Reserve System, Washington DC, US.; www.federalreserve.gov/publications/ACH-system/2013-discussion.html

89 Diaspora Bonds: Some Lessons for African Countries by Seliatou Kayode-Anglade and Nana Spio-Garbrah, *Africa Economic Brief,* Volume 3, Issue 13, African Development Bank, December 2012; www.afdb.org/fileadmin/uploads/afdb/Documents/Publications/Economic_Brief_-_Diaspora_Bonds_Some_Lessons_for_African_Countries.pdf

90 7th National Treasury of South Africa / OECD Forum on African Debt Management And Bond Markets, Procedures and Lessons on Issuance of Diaspora Bonds, 28 June 2013. Presenter: Rodney Mkansi , National Treasury Of South Africa; www.oecd.org/daf/fin/public-debt/14-SOUTH_AFRICA_RMkansi-Session5_Diaspora%20Bonds.pdf

91	Diaspora Bonds and Securitization of Remittances for Africa's Development, Abebe Shimeles, *Africa Economic Brief,* Volume 3, Issue 13, African Development Bank, December 2010; www.afdb.org/fileadmin/uploads/afdb/Documents/Publications/AEB%20dec%202010%20(avril%202011)_AEB%20dec%202010%20(avril%202011).pdf
92	*Understanding the Securitization of Worker Remittances* by Heather Hughes. American University, WCL Research Paper No. 2008-39. December 1, 2011; http://ssrn.com/abstract=1096700 or http://dx.doi.org/10.2139/ssrn.1096700
93	http://iom.ge/1/index.php
94	Borrowing Across Borders: Migration and Microcredit in Rural Cambodia by Maryann Bylander, *Development Viewpoint,* Number 74, School of Oriental and African Studies, Centre for Development Policy and Research, School of Oriental and African Studies, June 2014; www.soas.ac.uk/cdpr/publications/dv/file93549.pdf
95	*Philanthropy as an Emerging Contributor to Development Cooperation,* Heather Grady, Independent Philanthropy Advisor, July 2014. Commissioned by the United Nations Development Program as a Background Paper for the conference International Development Cooperation: Trends and Emerging Opportunities - Perspectives of the New Actors in Istanbul, June 2014; www.undp.org/content/dam/undp/documents/partners/civil_society/UNDP-CSO-philanthropy.pdf
96	*Millionaires and the Millennium: New Estimates of the Forthcoming Wealth Transfer and the Prospects for a Golden Age of Philanthropy,* Schervish, Paul G. and Havens, John J., Social Welfare Research Institute, Boston College, Boston, MA, October, 1999; *Why the $41 Trillion Wealth Transfer Estimate is Still Valid,* Schervish, Paul G. and Havens, John J., Social Welfare Research Institute, Boston College, Boston, MA, January 2003.And updated in 2011 www.bc.edu/content/dam/files/research_sites/cwp/pdf/A%20Golden%20Age%20of%20Philanthropy%20Still%20Bekons.pdf May 28, 2014
97	*Women and Philanthropy Boldly Shaping a Better World* by S. Shaw-Hardy and M. Taylor. John Wiley and Sons. 2010.
98	*The Wealth-X and Arton Capital Philanthropy Report 2014;* http://globalcitizen.org/wp-content/uploads/2014/10/WX_AC-Philanthropy-Report-2014-Web.pdf

99   *Preferences for International Redistribution.* C. Okten, and U. Osili. The World Bank. 2009.
100 *Generational Differences in Charitable Giving and in Motivations for Giving.* The Center on Philanthropy at Indiana University. Campbell and Company, 2008
101 *The Poor Give More* by Arthur C Brooks Portfolio.com, 2008.
102 Ibid.
103 *Something's Gotta Give – The State of Philanthropy in Asia;* The Economist Intelligence Unit, sponsored by HSBC Private Bank, 2011.
104 *Asia-Pacific Wealth Report, Capgemini and RBC Wealth Management. 2014;* www.uk.capgemini.com/thought-leadership/asia-pacific-wealth-report-2014-from-capgemini-and-rbc-wealth-management
105 *48 Heroes Of Philanthropy* by John Koppisch, Forbes Asia, July 2014; www.forbes.com/sites/johnkoppisch/2014/06/25/48-heroes-of-philanthropy-3
106 *Diaspora Philanthropy: Private Giving and Public Policy* by Kathleen Newland, Aaron Terrazas, and Roberto Munster. Migration Policy Institute. 2010; www.migrationpolicy.org/pubs/diasporas-philanthropy.pdf
107 *Women and Philanthropy Boldly Shaping a Better World.* S. Shaw-Hardy and M. Taylor. John Wiley and Sons, 2010.
108 Giving USA 2010; www.cfbroward.org/cfbroward/media/Documents/Sidebar%20Documents/GivingUSA_2010_ExecSummary_Print.pdf
109 CIA Factbook: www.cia.gov/library/publications/the-world-factbook/geos/bm.html
110 *World Giving Index 2014, A Global View of Giving Trends, Charities Aid Foundation,* November 2014; www.cafonline.org/about-us/publications/2014-publications/world-giving-index-2014
111 Ibid. – 98. http://global-citizen.org/building-a-center-for-hope/
112 *Philanthrocapitalism. How the Rich Can Save the World and Why We Should Let Them.* Matthew Bishop and Michael Green. London: A & C Black, 2008
113 Issues Note, UN Special Policy Dialogue on 'Private Philanthropic Organizations in International Development Cooperation: New Opportunities and Specific Challenges, Development Cooperation Forum, 7 February 2012; www.un.org/en/ecosoc/newfunct/pdf/dcf_philanthropy_issues_note.pdf
114 www.facebook.com/zuck/posts/10102507695055801

115 www.facebook.com/notes/mark-zuckerberg/a-letter-to-our-daughter/10153375081581634?pnref=story
116 *Portraits of Young Philanthropists: How Generation X and Generation Y are Transforming Charitable Giving.* The Economist Intelligence Unit, Fidelity Charitable Publication Date. Sep 17, 2014; www.economistinsights.com/sites/default/files/EIU_philanthropy_Sep15.pdf
117 'Measuring the Bang of Every Donated Buck', Alice Hohler. *Wall Street Journal online* March 1, 2010; www.wsj.com/articles/SB10001424052748703787304575075340954767332
118 The Changing Nature of Charity: Plugging in to the Digital Age by Kathleen Jolly. *Global News,* Canada. March 19, 2015; http://globalnews.ca/news/1881510/the-changing-nature-of-charity-plugging-in-to-the-digital-age; Young Tech Donors Take Leading Role in Philanthropy by Alex Daniels and Maria Di Mento. *The Chronicle of Philanthropy,* February, 8, 2015; https://philanthropy.com/article/Young-Tech-Donors-Take-Leading/151779
119 www.globalgiving.org/aboutus/
120 www.marketwired.com/press-release/crowdfunding-market-grows-167-2014-crowdfunding-platforms-raise-162-billion-finds-research-2005299.htm
121 Securitizing Philanthropy by Sean Stannard-Stockton. *Stanford Social Innovation review,* Oct. 24, 2008; http://ssir.org/articles/entry/securitizing_philanthropy#sthash.xqyIidF7.dpuf
122 www.schwabcharitable.org/public/charitable/about_schwab_charitable/news_pr/press_releases_archive/charitable_pioneers_microfinance.html
123 10 Innovations in Global Philanthropy. Concepts Worth Spreading in the UK. Plum Lomax and Rachel Wharton. *New Philanthropy Capital,* October 2014; www.thinknpc.org/wp-content/uploads/2014/10/10-innovations-in-global-philanthropy_FINAL.pdf; *GoodStart: A Social Investment Story,* prepared by Social Ventures Australia for the Australian Government Department of Education, Employment and Workplace Relations, 2012; http://socialventures.com.au/assets/Goodstart-report-Final.pdf
124 Coutts Fined for Failings in Money Laundering Controls, BBC News, 26 March 2012; www.bbc.co.uk/news/business-17512140
125 *From Charity to Social Change: Trends in Arab Philanthropy* by B. Ibrahim and D. Sharif. The American University in Cairo Press, 2008.

126 *Applying Behavioural Insights to Charitable Giving.* London: Cabinet Office, 28 May 2013; www.gov.uk/government/uploads/system/uploads/attachment_data/file/203286/BIT_Charitable_Giving_Paper.pdf
127 Ibid. -125.
128 USAID (Diaspora Philanthropy: Private Giving and Public Policy) 2010
129 www.gov.uk/international-development-funding/uk-aid-match
130 Ibid. 128.
131 Ibid. 128.
132 Ibid. 128.

Index

Abouchakra, Rabih, 16, 193
Abu Dhabi, 125, 170
accountability, 51–2, 59
active policies, 105, 110–19, 189
advance market commitments (AMCs), 170–71
Africare, 22–3
Agency for International Development (USAID), 20, 22–3, 118–19, 173
Agenda for Sustainable Development, 9–10
aid effectiveness, 39–41, 58
  harmonization and, 44–5
Aid Match, 169
aid programs, 19–38
  assistance-driven, 29–38
  changing landscape of, 23–4, 31–2, 71–2
  effectiveness, 39–42
    harmonization, 44–5
    role of recipient countries, 58
  historical evolution of, 24–5
    0.7 percent pledge, 27–8
    Green Revolution, 20–21
  investment driven, 30–31, 111–13, 147
  new donors, 32–4, 36–8
  synergy with philanthropic and remittance giving, 15–16, 184–5
  see also aid strategies; philanthropy; remittances
aid strategies, 43–70
  donor objectives, 43–4
    altruistic and cultural, 50–51

developmental, 1, 2, 9, 46–7
geopolitical, 48–50
humanitarian, 47–8
tied aid, 40, 66, 67–8
finance governance
  allocation, 63–8
  appropriation processes, 60, 62–3
  decentralized cooperation, 60–61
  disbursement, loans and grants, 66–8
  short-termism, 60
harmonization, 44–5
management approach, 51–63
  collaboration and cooperation, 54–8
  implementation/staffing, 58–60
  internal governance, accountable and flexible, 51–4, 61–2
monitoring and evaluation, 68–70
see also aid programs; philanthropy; remittances
Albert II, Prince of Monaco, 125
Alberta's Promise initiative, 165
allocation management, 63–6
  and disbursement, 66–8
Asia, 4, 5, 9, 20–21, 50, 65, 86, 87, 130, 132–3, 160, 183
assistance-driven aid programs, 29–38
Australasia, 130
Australia, 51, 53, 69, 86, 141, 157
Austria, 51

balance of payments, 78, 91, 112, 189
Bangladesh, 4, 87, 89, 92, 102, 108
banks, 108–9, 110, 113, 116, 122–3, 162
    World Bank, 8–9, 13, 25, 26, 81, 87, 89, 107, 171
Basu, Kaushik, 89
Behavioral Insight Team (BIT), 163–4
Belgium, 51
Bhutan, 141
bilateral and multilateral donations, 64, 144–5
Bill & Melinda Gates Foundation, 125, 170, 171
Brazil, 10, 30, 33, 35, 54, 85, 86
BRIC, 55
BRIMCK, 86
budget appropriations, 60, 62
Burkina Faso, 14, 93–4
Bylander, Maryann, 117

Cambodia, 117
Canada, 50, 51, 52, 54, 57, 62, 102, 141, 165, 169, 170, 171
Carter Center, 13, 146
cash, 147
centralization, 53
Chad, 21–3, 39
Chan Zuckerberg Initiative, 151–2
Charities Aid Foundation (CAF), 148, 164
charity outcomes, 143
Chen Feng, 133
child mortality rates, 3
China, 26, 30, 33, 35, 36–8, 44, 47, 54, 66, 67, 68, 71, 184
    donation figures, 133
    remittances, 87
Civil Society Organizations (CSO), 63
climate change, 4, 41
Clinton Global Initiative, 168
collaboration and cooperation, 44, 54–8, 186–7
collective remittances, 80, 90, 95–7, 122, 137, 189
Colombia, 58
Colonial Development Act, 24

Corporate Social Responsibility (CSR), 134
corruption, 39
Coutts and Co, 161–2
crowdfunding, 154–5

Danjuma, General Theophilus, 14
data collection, 109–10, 165
Dato Sri Tahir, 133
debt and debt relief, 8, 10, 40, 92, 111–12, 113, 117
decentralized cooperation, 60–61, 61
delivery channels, 63
demographic elements, 86–7
    migration patterns, 83–5
Denmark, 28, 46, 50, 51, 54, 56
Devarajan, Shanta, 9
Development Assistance Committee (DAC), 17, 32–4, 44
    China and, 36–8
    cooperative aid initiatives, 56–7
    field operations, 59–60
    funding, 60–8, 76
    governance models, 51, 53–4
    modern history of, 24–8
    monitoring and evaluation, 69
developmental aid, 1, 2, 46–7
    costs, 9
    Millennium Development Goals, 6–10, 28, 46, 126, 142
    'Transforming Our World: The 2030 Agenda for Sustainable Development', 7–8
    see also Official Development Assistance
disbursement, 66–8
disclosure and awareness, 106–7

Easterly, William, 40
Ebola, 4–5
Economist, The, 91, 152
education, 7, 40, 61, 65, 72, 84, 86, 92, 96, 137, 144, 153, 170, 173
Europe, migrants and remittance outflows, 86, 100
expatriate staff, 59

Facebook, 151–2
faith-based organizations (FBOs), 143, 144, 170
FedGlobal ACH, 110
Feng, Chen, 133
Financial Action Task Force on Money Laundering (FATF), 108
financial crisis (2008), 181
Finland, 28, 51
food security, 19–22
foreign direct investment (FDI), 82, 92, 143
foreign exchange reserves, 93
formal transfer systems, 97–9, 106–7, 189
foundations, 20, 25, 118, 125–6, 130, 135, 136–7, 142, 146, 148, 151–2, 170, 171, 173

Gallup's Worldview World Poll, 140
Gates Foundation, 125, 170, 171
geopolitical aid strategies, 48–50
Georgia, 116
Ghana, 112, 113, 133
GlamOnYou, 142
Global Citizen Foundation's Amal project, 142
global economy, 10
Global Partnership for Effective Development Co-operation, 58
Goodstart Consortium, 157
government interventions in remitter behaviour, 102–3, 105–6
　active policies, 105, 110–19, 189
　　investment encouragement, 111–13
　　microcredit programs, 117
　　migrant associations, support of, 114–15
　　retail payment/technical assistance, 115–6
　donor countries' involvement, 118–19
　passive policies, 105–10
　　banks, 108–9
　　data collection, 109–10
　　dialogue, 110
　　disclosure and awareness, 106–7
　　legislation and regulation, 107–8
　strategies, 121–4
　　governance models, 121–3
　　monitoring, 124
　　policies and programs, 123–4
　　set objectives, 121
governmental overarching strategy, 15, 184–6
　metrics and monitoring, 187–8
governments as philanthropists, 126–7, 134–5, 146, 155–75
　behavioral nudges, 163–4
　capacity building, 172–5
　co-financing, 167–72
　　advance market commitments (AMCs), 170–71
　　and impact evaluation, 171–2
　　innovation funds, 168
　　innovative forms, 155–7
　　matching fund programs, 169
　　resource-sharing, 170
　　zakat, 170
　determining objectives, 177–8
　financial innovation, social impact bonds, 155–7
　information supply, 164–7
　　on channels, outcomes and impacts, 166
　　on knowledge and data, 165
　　on priority issues, 166–7
　policy tools, 160
　regulation, 161–3
　　registration and licensing, 161–2
　　taxation, 162–3
　scope and role, 178–9
Grameen Bank, 148, 156
grants, 66
Greece, 51
Green Revolution, 20–21
Group 20 (G20) Small- and Medium-Size Enterprise Financing Challenge, 168

Haiti, 47, 50, 87, 102. 39
Hammami, Mona Hijazi, 191
harmonization, 44–5
Hawala, 100–101
health, 3, 4–5, 7, 12–14, 133, 170–71
Hewlett Foundation, 135
history of aid, 24–8
hometown associations (HTAs), 95, 96, 102, 115, 145, 173
Hudson Institute, 140
humanitarian aid strategies, 47–8
humanitarian outcomes, 142

illegal activities, 39, 94, 101, 108, 162
implementation of aid, 58–60
in-kind assistance, 67, 142
India, 21, 30, 35, 54, 71, 99, 133, 174
    remittances, 81, 85, 86, 87, 89, 108
        diaspora bonds, 112
        illegal activities and, 101, 108
individual remittances, 15, 95, 103
information supply, 164–7
innovation funds, 168
innovative forms of financing, 155–7
International Fund for Agricultural Development (IFAD), 116
International Monetary Fund (IMF), 25, 26, 191
internet, 154
investment driven aid, 30–31, 111–13, 147
Iran, 141
Ireland, 141
Israel, 112
Italy, 5, 51, 170, 171
iTunes, 142

Jamaica, 141
Jordan, 142

El Khoury, Michel, 16, 193
Kuraishi, Mari, 154

Lebanon, 92, 181
legislation and regulation, 107–8, 161–3
Liberia, 4–5, 39, 141

loans and grants, 66–7, 117, 148–9, 156
Luxembourg, 28, 51

Malta, 141
management approach to aid, 51–63
    collaboration and cooperation, 54–8
    financing, 60–63
    internal governance, accountable and flexible, 51–4, 61–2
    staffing, 58–60
Mari Kuraishi and Dennis Whittle, 154
Mastercard Foundation, 135
matching fund programs, 169
Maximum Philanthropic Benefit, 152–3
McNamara, Robert, 13
Mexico, 84, 85, 86, 96, 107, 110, 173
    Zacatecan migrants, 115
microcredit programs, 117, 148–9
Middle East, 9, 33, 86, 130, 135
migration *see* remittances
Millennium Development Goals (MDG), 6–10, 28, 46, 126, 142
Mo Ibrahim Foundation, 125
Mohammed bin Zayed Al-Nahyan, HH General Sheikh, 125
Moldovia, 97, 102
monitoring and evaluation, 68–70, 177–8
    social development as a metric, 173–4
Myanmar, 141

Nepal, 5, 87
Netherlands, 9, 12, 51, 53, 62, 63, 69
NextGenDonors, 152
NGOs, 59–60, 62–3, 76, 122, 143–4, 159–60, 173–5
    independence of, 159–60
Norway, 28, 51, 53, 54, 107, 171
nudge initiatives, 163–4

Official Development Assistance (ODA), 10–11, 19, 24, 25–6, 28, 31–7, 143
    activity and functions, 182
    donation figures, 31–4, 140
    see also developmental aid

INDEX 211

Onchocerciasis Control Program, 12–14
Organization for Economic Cooperation (OECD), 25, 27, 29, 37, 61, 84, 86, 140, 153
  DAC *see* Development Assistance Committee (DAC)

Pakistan, 4, 48, 49, 101, 108, 175
passive policies, 105–10
philanthropy
  activity and functions, 11, 139–41, 182
    World Giving Index (WGI), 140–41
  awareness raising, 165–7
  channels, intermediaries or direct, 143–6
  corporations, foundations and governments, 134–6
    motivations, 136–7
  forms and outcomes, 141–3
  individuals, 130–34
    age disparity, 131–2
    donors, 132–3
    education and income levels, 132
    gender disparity, 130–31
    motivation, 136–7
  new generation of donors, 151–3
  new models, 153, 177–9
    government objectives, scope and role, 177–9
    nudge initiatives, 163–4
    strategic/'Smart,' 160
    venture philanthropy, 153
  new technologies, 154–5
  operating model distinctions, 173–5
  scope of, 125–7
  synergy with aid and remittance giving, 15–16, 184–5
  visibility, measuring impact, 152–3, 171–2
  work force training, 172–3
  see also aid programs; aid strategies; remittances
Philippines, 91, 92, 107, 133
0.7 percent pledge, 27–8
policy statements, 53

population growth, 5–6
Portugal, 51
poverty, 3, 6

Razon, Enrique, 133
Red Cross, 142
refugees, 5
regulation, governmental, 107–8, 161–3
religious bodies, 143, 144, 170
remittances, 81–7
  activity and functions, 11, 182
  advantages of, 89–92
  collective, 80, 90, 95–7, 122, 137, 189
    hometown associations (HTAs), 96
  disadvantages of, 93–4, 183–4
  financial transfer figures (2014), 2
  financial transfer mechanisms, 97–102
    credit unions, 99, 106, 107
    diaspora bonds, 111–13
    formal systems, 97–9, 106–7
      banks, 97, 99, 108–9
      Special Purpose Vehicle (SPV), 113
    informal systems, 100–102
      Hawala system, 100–101
    innovation in, 116
    new technologies for, 115–16
  government intervention, 102–3, 105–19
    active policies, 105, 110–19, 189
    host countries' involvement, 118–19
    passive policies, 105–10
    strategies, 121–4
  individual, 15, 95, 103
  major recipient countries, 87
  microfinancing and, 117
  migrant associations, 114–15
  migration patterns and, 83–5
  remittance flows, 85–7
    data collection, 109–10
    figures, 11
    from middle-income and developing countries, 86
    significance of, 119
  synergy with aid and philanthropy, 15–16, 184–5

see also aid programs, aid strategies; philanthropy

sanitation, 4, 115
Schwab Charitable microfinance guarantee program, 156
securitization, 113
social development as a metric, 173–4
social impact bonds, 155–6
social inequality, 93
social initiatives, nudging, 163–4
social return on investment, 153
SOHO Foundation, 135
South Korea, 33, 58, 85, 86
south–north migration, 84–5, 190
south–south migration, 83–4, 190
Spain, 5, 51, 61, 86, 172
Special Purpose Vehicle (SPV), 113
Sri Lanka, 108, 141
staffing, 58–60, 172–3
stakeholders, 8, 186–7
structured finance, 126, 156–7, 171
Sub-Saharan Africa, 4, 5, 12, 21, 65
Sunstein, Cass, 163
Swales Foundation, 135
Sweden, 28, 51, 65–6
Switzerland, 28, 51, 53, 59, 66
synergy of giving, 15–16, 184–5
Syria, 5, 34, 47, 142

Tahir, Dato Sri, 133
Tajikistan, 81, 87, 89, 141
technologies, 115–16, 154–5
Thailand, 117, 141
Thaler, Richard, 163
tied aid, 40, 66, 67–8
Tinbergen, Jan, 27
Tobago, 141
'Transforming Our World: The 2030 Agenda for Sustainable Development', 7–8
transparency, 152–3, 161
    accountability, 51–2, 59
    monitoring outcomes, 68–70, 177–8, 183–4
    social development as a metric, 173–4
triangular cooperation, 56–7

Trinidad, 141
Turkey, 86, 108–9

Uganda, 4, 102
undernourished people, 6
United Kingdom of Great Britain, 51
    banking security concerns, 161–2
    Department for International Development (DFID), 53
    matching fund programs, 169
    multilateral aid strategy, 66, 118
    nudge initiatives, 163–4
    social impact bonds, 155
United Nations, 27, 63, 65, 144
    Millennium Development Goals, 6–10, 28, 46, 126, 142
United States, 51
    Agency for International Development (USAID), 20, 22–3, 118–19, 173
    contributions to Millennium Development Goals, 125–6
    migrants and remittance outflows, 86, 100, 102, 110, 118–19
    philanthropic giving, 2, 125–6, 130, 139–41, 143
        co-financing, 168
    President's Science Advisory Committee, 20
    social impact bonds, 156

venture philanthropy, 153
Vietnam, 50, 86, 173

Warwick-Ching, Lucy, 152–3
water supply, 4, 7–8, 21–3, 46, 56
wealth distribution, 3
Wellcome Trust, 135
Whittle, Dennis, 154
work force, 58–60, 172–3
World Bank, 8–9, 13, 25, 26, 81, 87, 89, 107, 171
World Economic Forum, 168
World Giving Index (WGI), 140–41
World Health Organization, 3, 12, 25
Wouterse, Fleur, 93–4